Scenes Of Glory

Subplots Of God's Long Story

David O. Bales

CSS Publishing Company, Inc., Lima, Ohio

SCENES OF GLORY

Copyright © 2008 by
CSS Publishing Company, Inc.
Lima, Ohio

All rights reserved. No part of this publication may be reproduced in any manner whatsoever without the prior permission of the publisher, except in the case of brief quotations embodied in critical articles and reviews. Inquiries should be addressed to: Permissions, CSS Publishing Company, Inc., 517 South Main Street, Lima, Ohio 45804.

Scripture quotations are from the New Revised Standard Version of the Bible, copyright 1989 by the Division of Christian Education of the National Council of the Churches of Christ in the USA. Used by permission.

Library of Congress Cataloging-in-Publication Data

Bales, David O., 1948-
   Scenes of glory : subplots of God's long story / David O. Bales.
   p. cm.
   Includes index.
   ISBN 0-7880-2554-6 (perfect bound : alk. paper)
   1. Christian life. 2. Bible—Meditations. I. Title.

BV4515.3.B35 2008
252—dc22

2008018904

For more information about CSS Publishing Company resources, visit our website at www.csspub.com or email us at csr@csspub.com or call (800) 241-4056.

Cover design by Barbara Spencer
ISBN-13: 978-0-7880-2554-9
ISBN-10: 0-7880-2554-6

PRINTED IN USA

Foreword

In *Scenes Of Glory*, Presbyterian pastor and writer, David O. Bales has written a wonderful book in service to the church, people of faith, and people who may continue to wonder why faith matters in the first place. Early in his introduction, the author gives his readers an important clue as to the purposes of these stories, his stories, and our stories. Bales reminds us that the story of the "wandering Aramean" in Deuteronomy 26 is his story, and our story, too. People of faith are often wandering, that is, often alien, often seemingly few in number, often laboring in untenable circumstances but always, always, part of a larger narrative: God's story, God's plan for each one of us. That is, of course, one of the many gifts of holy scripture. Through a process of reading and comprehending, the give-and-take of narrative and narrative imagination, we are but a living extension of the Bible's grand narrative: timeless themes of lostness, foundness, sin, salvation, and grace, always surrounded by God's eternal love and commitment. We, in the words of master storyteller, Frederick Buechner, know that "... the journey is our home."

I am confident that your journey through *Scenes Of Glory* will be a tangible reminder that, indeed, we are part of that larger narrative of salvation history. Thanks be to God!

> The Reverend Doctor Jeffrey F. Bullock
> President of University of Dubuque
> Author of *Preaching with a Cupped Ear*

Preface

Instead of spending time in an introduction justifying and explaining the whys and hows of stories in church, the introduction is a sermon to be modified and preached by others.

All of these stories were originally read in worship. Every chapter includes Discussion Questions. Therefore, this volume has a dual function. The stories are suitable for public worship and also, with the Discussion Questions, are curriculum for group discussion.

In my first book, *Gospel Subplots: Story Sermons Of God's Grace*, I thanked many people who encouraged and helped me to write. Following is a list of others from across the years who have encouraged my writing, read my manuscripts, given their critiques, or supplied facts needed for stories. I thank you all.

Hugh Anderson (with "oh en"), Sandy Ashby (who helped on most of these stories), Dave Bartlett, Sherrill Boyd, Earl Burkholder, Donna Clark, Tom Clarke, John Courtney, Harry Cronin, Denise Currin, Eva Dickson, Jack and Shirley Dow, Rodrigo Duarte (my son-in-law), Ivan and Jan Ellis, Helen Faries, Todd Flocchini, Joe and Cathy Foran, Ron and Mary Fredrickson, Dennis and Lynn Gish, Wayne and Betty Helland, Haldane and Pat Harris, Jim Hudson, Verlyn and Marian Iverson, Ben Johnson, John Kleeman, Valeree Lane, Lance Lesueur, Bev McCluskey, Mary Olson, Jim and Laura Stewart, Dorothy Stow (my sister), Barry Watts, Dick and Nancy Wendt, Ken Winter (who is as faithful as a brother)

Some of the stories have previously been published in the online clergy journal "StoryShare." They are used here by permission.

The church is a story-formed community. Praise be to God.

— David O. Bales

Table Of Contents

Introduction	11
Scenes Of Glory: The Bible's Long Story	
Acts 7:2-53; Deuteronomy 26:1-11	
Chapter 1	19
Dancing In Eden's Airport	
Genesis 2:7, 18-25	
Chapter 2	27
Do This	
Exodus 12:1-4, 11-14	
Chapter 3	31
Mid Cemetery	
2 Samuel 1:1-17	
Chapter 4	35
Solomon's Prayer	
1 Kings 8:22-30, 42-43	
Chapter 5	39
Unanswerable	
Job 38:1-7	
Chapter 6	43
O People Walking In Darkness	
Isaiah 9:2	
Chapter 7	51
The Twins	
Hosea 11:3	
Chapter 8	57
The Chief Magi's Son	
Matthew 2:1-12	
Chapter 9	61
July Fifth	
Matthew 5:38-39	
Chapter 10	75
By What Authority?	
Mark 1:21-28	
Chapter 11	79
Jerusalem From The West	
Mark 1:40-44; Psalm 125:2; Isaiah 53:7-8	

Chapter 12 **Althea Genler's Subtle Memorial Blessing** *Mark 4:10-12; Jude 24-25*	89
Chapter 13 **Jesus' Questions** *Mark 9:30-37*	101
Chapter 14 **Gravensteins** *Mark 12:28-34*	105
Chapter 15 **Collision Course To The Cross** *Mark 15:21-26*	109
Chapter 16 **Rich And Poor Alike?** *Luke 6:17-26*	117
Chapter 17 **Signs** *Luke 21:25-36*	121
Chapter 18 **Third Voice In The Courtyard** *Luke 22:54-66*	125
Chapter 19 **Joseph Of Arimathea And Of Jerusalem** *Luke 23:50-56*	133
Chapter 20 **The Whole Truth** *Luke 24:36-48*	141
Chapter 21 **The True Israelite** *John 1:43-51; Genesis 28:10-12*	145
Chapter 22 **Upside Down** *John 2:13-22*	153
Chapter 23 **Fifty Feet Below Molly's Face** *John 3:6-8; Isaiah 9:6*	157
Chapter 24 **And What Else?** *John 6:1-21*	167

Chapter 25	171
Lazarus: Second Death, Third Life	
John 11:1-13, 38-44	
Chapter 26	179
John's Final Revision	
John 21:20-25; John 14:18; John 16:13	
Chapter 27	185
The Seminarian	
1 Corinthians 2:12	
Chapter 28	191
Setting: Corinth, Greece, 55 AD	
1 Corinthians 8:1-13	
Chapter 29	199
What A Rotten Text For Today	
1 Corinthians 13	
Chapter 30	205
Search For The True Believer	
2 Corinthians 11:29	
Chapter 31	213
Languishing Legend	
Galatians 3:28	
Chapter 32	223
How Are Things In Guanajuato?	
Ephesians 3:14-19	
Chapter 33	229
Team Bus	
Ephesians 4:15-16	
Chapter 34	237
Doctor Of Divinity	
1 Peter 5:1-4	
Chapter 35	245
The Most Faithful Nonbeliever	
1 John 3:11	
Chapter 36	253
Seeing The End	
Revelation 1:4b-8	
Scripture Index	257
Emphasis Or Special Occasion Index	259

Introduction

Scenes Of Glory: The Bible's Long Story

Acts 7:2-53; Deuteronomy 26:1-11

I grew up a quarter mile from Ralph Waldo Emerson. Not the one whose "Self-Reliance" you had to read in high school. This Ralph Emerson, however, had more influence upon me than the author. I didn't know that his middle name was Waldo until later in my life. He seemed really old — must have been sixty. He was a logger in his youth.

I remember Ralph Emerson and my dad in the summers at least once a week in our front yard under the apple tree sitting on top of the picnic table. They talked about everything from logging to fishing to politics. One afternoon as we sat there, Ralph told about his leaving logging camp, going to town, and getting drunk. He was so drunk that he had to hold onto a mule's tail to pull him two miles back to camp. He said he never drank like that again. When he left, Dad said to me, "He told that story for your sake."

"What?" I asked.

"So you'd learn from his experience and not to do the same thing."

In Acts 6, Stephen is arrested, charged with blasphemy, and arraigned before the Jewish council. In Acts 7, the chief priest asks the accused whether the charges are true. Stephen doesn't present what we expect of a courtroom defense. In those times, the speech of the accused could support the cause he represented. Stephen presents a panoramic view of the long and convoluted story of the Hebrew people for our sake. He selects stories from the Old Testament to help us learn and live. We do this not only by being informed by them, but also by becoming involved in them.

The Jewish councillors who hear Stephen's recitation know the history already. Stephen isn't telling them anything new. But knowing a story already doesn't make it meaningless or boring. We know many stories word for word. We can hear Lou Gehrig saying that he is the luckiest man in the world. We can recall FDR's naming one day "a date that will live in infamy." I looked forward to seeing my friend, Jim, at denominational events and sharing a meal with him. He usually broke up the restaurant with his joking. I always asked him to tell about the three sleeping bags after the disastrous camping trip. (It involved a urine sample!) Katherine Hankey's gospel hymn, "I Love To Tell The Story," expresses the same longing to hear the good news of Christ. Her third verse begins,

> *I love to tell the story;*
> *For those who know it best*
> *Seem hungering and thirsting*
> *To hear it, like the rest.*[1]

"Some researchers into the human brain have concluded that it reasons not by analyzing data, but by recalling stories. We have cultural stories in the very fabric of our thinking ... and those stories influence what we notice in a given situation, how we interpret it, and how we choose to react."[2] The stories families pass on with tears of joy or sorrow explain where we've come from and who we are. On a larger scale, our stories of an ethnic group or nation clarify who we are and why we're here, from the Jamestown settlement in 1607 AD to the Hebrew slaves escaping Egypt in the thirteenth century BC. Humans have always lived as much by stories as by rational explanations. We form our deepest commitments both by conceptual understanding and by stories that we believe explain not only life in general, but also indicate who we are, where we've come from, and where we're going.

Every four years at national political conventions, speakers remind their allies about *their* presidents, and the roll is called over the decades and the stories of their party's accomplishments are recited to the roars and claps of those who not only believe that such statements are at least half-true, but who also have committed effort and money to support the party. When these stories are chanted, they aren't experienced as the record of people long ago and far away. They're the stories of who we are. Most of the history recounted at political conventions could have occurred before we were born, but it's our story.

I'd been a Christian for ten years and was a pastor. I took a graduate class at Seattle University. It was an interactive, some would say "touchy-feely," class. In our first meeting, the instructor said, "I'll give you a few minutes to think and then I'd like each of you to tell about your family of origin and how that family has made you who you are and brought you to where you are."

As I prepared to tell about my family and who I was, I realized for the first time that I couldn't explain myself anymore just by my birth family, but only by the larger family of faith in the Old and New Testaments. I, with the indulgence of the class, told of my faith by quoting Deuteronomy 26, "A wandering Aramean was my ancestor; he went down into Egypt and lived there as an alien, few in number, and there he became a great nation, mighty and populous. When the Egyptians treated us harshly and afflicted us, by imposing hard labor on us, we cried to the Lord, the God of our ancestors" (Deuteronomy 26:5b-7a).

That's the basic faith of the Hebrew people into which you and I have been adopted as Christians. The story recited in this scripture explains not only who the Hebrews were and how they ended up in Israel, but also who you and I are and who got us to where we are. Deuteronomy 26, as does Stephen in his New Testament speech, hits a few of the highlights and turning points of Hebrew history, especially the harrowing tasks in slavery to Egypt. It asserts that God rescued the Hebrew people from Egypt and brought them to a new life in the land of Canaan. Both the Old and New Testaments are based upon God's grace to us. Add all the stories together and you see that first God saves us, then God tells us how to live — and not the other way around.

When you come to such prescriptive statements as the Bible's Ten Commandments in Exodus 20, you arrive prepared for the Bible's demands by the good news of the Bible's stories in Exodus

1 through 19 — as opposed to the Sunday school teacher who put off preparing his lesson. On Saturday night he decided the children the next day should study the Ten Commandments. He skipped the stories of God's rescuing the Hebrew people from slavery and went right to the Ten Commandments, cleanly missing all the understanding and motivation for God's people to trust God and to obey the Ten Commandments.

We form our deepest commitments not so much by grasping abstract explanations as by being grasped by stories that explain life and us. For church school teachers, whether teachers of children or adults, our first task isn't to urge our pupils, "Let's all be nice to one another." Our first task is to repeat the Bible's story, the sad parts as well as the happy ones. Let our students hear the breadth of the scriptures so they can begin to understand the depths.

Throughout the book of Acts, the new Christian church grows when people gather and hear the story of what God has finally done through Jesus. They trust God and join the fellowship of believers. The variations in the four gospels show that Jesus' story was told different ways to different people in different times and places. But always the church is a story-formed community — it has been since the beginning and still is.

My part of the Church with a capital "C" is the Presbyterian Church (USA), the church with a small "c." Presbyterians can recall the stories of faith that have formed us: Richard Haklyt, the English preacher who pushed to colonize the new world; and the French Huguenots who tried to do so in Florida; and the Puritans at Plymouth who were marginally successful. We recall the Dutch Reformed and the Scotch-Irish and the Highland Scots who immigrated here with a Presbyterian slant to the faith.

Our story includes Francis Makemie, imprisoned for preaching without a license in colonial New York; and the Tennant family, whose log cabin college began Princeton University; and John Witherspoon, who later became president of Princeton and who was the only clergyman to sign the Declaration of Independence. We each could continue to tell the stories of missionaries and pastors, lay people and teachers whose lives and ministries affected us directly. We could just as well recite the same kinds of stories for

Methodists, Baptists, Lutherans, Eastern Orthodox, or Roman Catholics. I'm being selective by mentioning Presbyterians. Stephen was selective in his sermon, also. Whichever branch of Christ's church we recall, we don't do so in order to praise Christians, but to honor God. As with the stories in the Bible, in the stories of our own Christian heritage we hear what God did through and in spite of people like us and we turn in gratitude to God.

The Bible's stories aren't static but dynamic. They aren't once and for all statements. Within our various branches of Christ's church we continue to hear the Bible's stories and to find new meaning in them. They're active expressions of God's living grace. Passing through the centuries and through our souls, the Bible's message becomes fuller and richer to each new generation that hears them. It's a jaw-dropping, heart-speeding, feet-moving story, an overarching, multifaceted, interconnected story intended to include us. It's aimed toward us, to pull us into God's gracious realm so that God's cause in Jesus Christ might become the cause and way of life for everyone.

God's choice to use stories in the Bible isn't a second-rate compromise for how to communicate truth to us. The Bible's stories have supported faith for 4,000 years. If our hearing a story seems a simplistic or mediocre way to be affected by the Christian faith, then a test: I guess that most readers (listeners) will leave this chapter (sermon) with at least two things. You remember my father and Ralph Emerson talking under an apple tree as they sat on what? (picnic table). Certainly you remember Ralph Emerson's two-mile trip back to logging camp grasping what? (mule's tail). You remember these because they occur in a story of people like yourselves, people like those Stephen tells about, people through whom God works (and the Bible proclaims that God only has people like us to work with). You remember the events in my childhood story, unless, of course, you were distracted, because you are still waiting to hear what happened to the three sleeping bags after my friend, Jim's, disastrous camping trip — and you want to know how the urine sample fits into that story.

We remember stories and we want to hear stories — not just funny stories, but stories where our faith and life are portrayed in the drama of the spoken word. The Bible's stories teach us at the deepest level that God won't give us up. God won't leave this world to its own devices and won't leave us alone, either.

The Bible's stories speak to us and win our attention. They immerse us in God's deep, eternal love. The Bible's events — the ones Stephen includes in his speech and the ones he skips — aren't told primarily to entertain us or to inform us, or even to involve us, but to transform us. God has told the Bible's long story for your sake. God's stories change our thinking and our behavior, because as we hear them they change who we are and where we've ultimately come from. They help us raise our voices in God's praise, completing Katherine Hankey's last verse:

And when, in scenes of glory,
I sing the new, new song,
'Twill be the old, old story
That I have loved so long.[3]

---

1. "I Love To Tell The Story," words by Katherine Hankey, circa 1868. In the public domain.

2. Nancy Kress, *Dynamic Characters* (Cincinnati: Writer's Digest Books, 1998), pp. 225-226.

3. *Op cit*, Hankey.

Discussion Questions

1. Is/was your family one that passed on family stories?

2. What's the earliest story you remember hearing in your family? What's the story your family told most often as you grew up?

3. Are you a person who lives more by stories or concepts? When do stories affect you more than concepts?

4. What difference does it make that the Bible isn't always telling us what to do or not to do but that the majority of the Bible reports God's working with people like us?

5. What kind of stories in the Bible and the Christian faith are you most drawn to or repelled by?

6. What are your favorite Old Testament stories or New Testament stories?

7. If you were Stephen, what story from the Old Testament would you add to the speech? What story would you delete from the speech?

8. In the Christian faith, what can stories best communicate? For what and when must the Christian faith use other forms of communication?

9. What stories of faith would you substitute for those that have been mentioned from the Presbyterian tradition?

10. Do you have a "holy" story that you would share with others now?

Emphasis or special occasion: Marriage

Chapter 1

Dancing In Eden's Airport

Genesis 2:7, 18-25

If it wasn't for Ellen, Glen thought. He clenched his jaw so tightly he began to worry about his bridgework. *Must relax, can't put out another $3,000 on teeth, let alone the time and pain in a dentist's chair.*

If it wasn't for Ellen, he said that to himself with increasing frequency in the last four-and-a-half years. Bad enough that Ellen's condition led her, now weekly, to a group that should be named "let's all share our humiliation," but was called, instead, "support." Now, because of Ellen, here he was listening to inanity if not downright blasphemy.

Ellen said, "If I'm going to attend their group, we ought to attend their worship."

No wonder she was depressed — thinking she always owed something to others. Instead of being prisoners merely to her depression, they now became prisoners in worship: singing songs they didn't know, trying to imitate others — figuring out when to stand, sit, or kneel. The preacher was a child who'd probably been shaving for only six months, which was also when he got his last haircut. But here he was, prancing across the front of the church, dressed like a Byzantine prince. He kept saying, "Friends...." Friends this and friends that. *He's not my friend,* Glen thought.

It didn't help that they were sitting beside Horseface and Moonface. Glen's full names for them were: Horseface/Clubfoot and Moonface/Sticklegs. Somehow, this pair felt it necessary to accompany Glen and Ellen everywhere. The couple hosted Glen and Ellen to dinner, and twice Horseface phoned Glen to go to lunch. Glen looked at the two. He named the husband Horseface/

Clubfoot, because he had a longish face with a high forehead and a lock of coarse, curly, red hair always bobbing in front. With his left foot turned outward, even in a suit he was as awkward as an ostrich dancing a minuet. His wife, Moonface/Sticklegs, had a wide, asymmetrical face and a knobby nose. She seemed all knees and elbows. Like an adolescent who grew eight inches in a summer, her every movement seemed to flop like a marionette. As Glen glanced at the two of them sitting next to him and Ellen, it struck him: They're assigned to us. We're their project!

Then the capping indignity. The child preacher, ironically called "Father," reeled out the longest line of baloney Glen ever heard. Glen was simply dumbfounded that such nonsense was allowed for a sermon, though the program named it a "homily." Not as though he knew a lot about the Bible, but he went to Sunday school when he was a boy and knew you shouldn't play cute with the Holy Book. From the pulpit, the child-father said, "Adam's initial experience was God's blowing through his lips the first breath a human would ever breathe. God suscitated, not resuscitated, Adam. One moment a pile of mud, and the next a person powered by amino acids, with cells built around endoplasmic reticulum, and equipped with a set of teeth ready to start decaying.

"God presented animals for Adam to name, as a parent brings pets to an only child, but no animal was adequate. Then God anesthetized him and pulled the start of a woman right out of Adam's side.

"The first time Adam's lips touched Eve's, it was like the sensation of God's touching his lips, but more fun. Adam often lay awake to ponder Eve while she slept — her sinuses made her snore. Even when asleep, Eve wanted to stay near where her rib came from, so if her knees weren't in his back, she was breathing in his face. When she breathed upon his face, he thought of God's breath upon him.

"Adam had only glimpsed God's face once. As the memory faded and Adam sought to recall that first breath, he beheld a face more and more like Eve's.

"Is this exactly what the Genesis story means? To a small degree, yes; because Adam and Eve are part of us all. Since God's image is in all of us, you should be able to glimpse something of God, when you look into the face of the spouse you love."

Glen expected church officials to swarm the young man and smite him with fists and chairs. Yet no one charged toward him. Perhaps since they insisted he be celibate, the congregation indulged his fantasies.

As they filed out of the church, people laughed with the young man or slapped his shoulder. A few women hugged him. Horseface/Clubfoot and Moonface/Sticklegs, also known as Wes and Lois Torgeson, stepped up to Father Harry and presented Glen and Ellen. Glen merely said, "Hello." If it wasn't for Ellen!

On the drive home, he said, "I was so angry, being trapped into hearing such a thing."

Ellen said, "I didn't mind." There were more and more things lately she didn't mind or wouldn't set her mind to. When they married eleven years before, Ellen was a beautiful and bright person. Glen described her recent deterioration as her emotions pulling the plug on her intelligence, but only to himself. She sat around most of the day. If she went out, she often locked her keys in the car. She didn't prepare supper on time and if she did, left the dishes unwashed. Whatever he left her to do when he departed for work in the morning, even the simplest thing, something of it wouldn't be done in the evening. Glen took over writing their bills and returning letters. If pots sat soaking more than two days, he washed them. When he got down to his last clean underwear, he washed clothes. He pondered about the house: *Come spring, I suppose I'll have to scrub the windows.*

Wes phoned on Tuesday morning. He was flying overseas for a while and wouldn't be able to have lunch with Glen this week. "But if you and Ellen need anything, don't hesitate to call Lois."

"Phone a woman? I find the woman I'm around pretty unreliable." Glen laughed. Wes didn't.

"Could I bring you something from England?" Wes asked.

"England? Really? Well, you know, it's kind of funny, but I'd really like a horse brass. Could you get me one?"

"You mean an antique?"

"No, just a tourist trinket. You could probably pick up one in a shop at Heathrow."

"Right-o," Wes said with a British accent. "I'll keep praying for you guys, and I'll do my best to get you a horse brass."

"Sure," Glen said and hung up. *If you don't trip over your own feet trying*, he thought to himself.

In the next two weeks, Ellen's condition worsened. She saw her medical doctor each week and her counselor every other day. Lois phoned most evenings and on Wednesday brought a full dinner for them.

"Thank you," Glen said, when she placed the Chiquita® bananas box full of food on the kitchen table.

"No problem," Lois said, and she smiled broadly. For the first time, she seemed pretty — and so healthy. From the window, he watched her leave. *Not much for legs, but the rest of her is all right.*

On Sunday Ellen wasn't well enough to attend worship, but the next Sunday she said they'd go no matter how she felt. Father Harry wasn't quite as flippant. Lois sat beside Ellen. Glen breathed more freely once he was outside the church. Ellen and Lois talked about their group. Lois said, "Wes'll be home tomorrow or Tuesday."

"You don't know which?" Ellen asked.

"He's trying to get out as soon as he can, but it all depends upon seven or eight people filing reports on time."

"I bet you really miss him," Ellen said.

"Ohhh," she said, "I'll be so relieved when he gets home."

As Glen and Ellen walked to their car, Glen glanced back at Lois hurrying into the church. *Yes, except for spindly legs, not bad.*

That night, as Glen and Ellen were getting ready for bed, the phone rang. Glen scrambled out of the bathroom, toothbrush in hand, to answer. It was Lois.

"I'm sorry to bother you, Glen. I must've been in the laundry room and didn't hear the phone. I just found a message on the answering machine. I can't make it all out. Somebody with a really thick English accent says Wes is on a plane, but then there was static. They said United, but I couldn't catch the number or what city he was transferring in."

"Cool down," Glen said. "Whatever plane he's on, he'll phone when he gets in."

"I know he could. But I've got this problem about flying. I can't get in ... I can't get in a plane and I worry terribly about people flying. I've always met Wes at every plane. It's really important to me."

"I don't see the problem," Glen said. "But you can just go to the airport and wait. Hang around the baggage return. Everybody has to come there. You can't miss him."

"That's kind of what I'd like to do. But I can't start my car. Wes said the celluloid was acting up."

"Solenoid," Glen said.

"Yes. But it won't start, no matter what I try." She paused, "Could you ... it's a lot to ask, I know. Could you try to start it?"

Glen hesitated, then, "Yeah. Sure. I'll be right over."

Lois turned the key while Glen jiggled wires under the hood. But after ten minutes he said, "I'm not much of a mechanic. I can't get the blessed thing to run."

"It's not your fault." Her voice was tight. "And I'm sorry I phoned you so late. I get panicky about flying."

"I'll take you to the airport."

"Oh, no, no. You've done enough. I've calmed down, honest. I'll call a cab. I'm okay. Really."

"Come on. I'll get you there. I owe you one. Hop in."

The tension in Lois's face faded and was replaced by a beautiful smile.

"All right. I appreciate it. I'll get my purse."

Although Glen had been sleepy when Lois phoned, he now felt wide awake. Lois was strikingly dressed — pink suit with matching purse. Even her hair was done up nicely. He couldn't help looking sideways at her. Together as relative strangers it felt like a date.

They didn't say much. The traffic became dangerous near the stadium. A doubleheader had gone into extra innings and now fans were dashing home, making Glen concentrate more upon driving than upon Lois. When traffic cleared, he noticed she held her left hand on the seat between them. Was this an invitation or at least an intimation that she wanted to be near him? Did she feel the same things he felt? After all, she did phone him.

About two miles from the airport, he reached over and put his hand upon hers. She smiled at him and didn't move away. As they came into sight of the airport, Lois pulled her hand slowly from under his, patted him, and said, "Wes and I made it through depression. You and Ellen will, too."

Glen coughed and put both hands on the wheel.

He hadn't been to the airport since its three-year remodeling project. The newspaper reported the mayor praising the airport authority for finishing the project before the end of 1999. Speaking in what Glen called his "usual double-talk," the mayor said, "Our airport prepares us for the next millennium. It's the place where the past meets the future and the future arrives early."

The outside lights aimed strategically upon thin spires and spidery flying buttresses. He parked on the third level and they walked past the dimly lit rows of rental cars and through the airport's giant doors. The doors opened automatically as if to welcome them into the light. Glen was staggered at the architecture: high, majestic, vaulted ceilings.

They found the United television monitors for arriving flights. "I can make it from here," Lois said.

"You sure? I could stay."

"I'm fine. There aren't that many incoming flights."

"Okay, if you're sure."

They shook hands. Lois continued down the corridor and Glen stepped into the restroom. As he exited the restroom, Lois dashed past on the other side of the corridor. She was in a crowd and didn't see him. She was hurrying, which made her look more ungainly. She appeared worried; but he let her go. She was an adult.

He watched her encounter a swarm of arriving passengers, their clothes wrinkled from having flown at least a third of the way around the globe. Then Wes appeared from behind a pillar. Lois was passing immediately in front of him as he threw out his left arm to catch her by the waist. Her right leg flew up as he lifted her and swung her around in a pirouette as graceful as though they practiced ballet three hours a day. Lois squealed and grasped her arms around his neck. He swung her around twice, as they disregarded the people near them.

Glen was fifty feet away. He stopped mid-stride when he saw Wes lift Lois. They seemed to move in slow motion. He wondered if two people ever danced in a more elegant display. He backed away, transfixed by the spinning couple, and he bumped into a woman talking on a cell phone. It was hard to stop looking at Wes and Lois. He watched them hugging and laughing, then he turned to depart before they noticed him. He almost tripped as he slinked away with his head low. He felt as though he had somehow stumbled into the holiest place on earth where he had no right to be.

Discussion Questions

1. What immediate responses do you have to the story?

2. Do you identify with a character in the story? If yes, how and why do you identify with the person? If no, why don't you identify with anyone in the story?

3. Would you like to have a conversation with a character in the story? What would you say, ask, or suggest to the person? Why?

4. How does the story bring the biblical text into a clearer focus for you?

5. How would you improve or modify the story? Why?

6. Have you been offended by a worship service or sermon? Has your opinion of that service changed? How? Why? Why not?

7. Have you reflected upon the meaning of God's making male and female? Is this a reality that is important to your faith?

8. Has the love between a man and woman you know helped your faith in God?

9. What further depths of meaning, symbols, connections with, or applications of the biblical faith do you find in the story?

10. Since Jesus Christ has risen from the dead and is alive among us through his Holy Spirit, what of this story would you like Christ to activate in your life?

Emphasis or special occasion: Maundy (Holy) Thursday

Chapter 2

Do This

Exodus 12:1-4, 11-14

"I'm telling you what the Lord told Aaron and me," Moses said. "Now is the decisive moment. This time we'll gain our freedom; and, we're commanded to prepare for it by a meal. I've told you the particulars. It's not difficult." But as Moses repeated this, he felt the same resistance as when he'd said it the first time to these Hebrew field-workers. He'd gathered them near their village at twilight as they returned home from tending Egypt's crops.

Men stood back from the Lord's two leaders. They knew Moses and Aaron well, and listened respectfully. This pair of fellows had brought them a great deal of grief — having to work harder, bricks without straw — because these two had marched right into Pharaoh's court and demanded he release the Hebrew workers.

Well, these Hebrews were exhausted. They'd toiled at Egypt's building projects and in Egypt's fields, they had been harassed, bullied, and maltreated until they felt only a breath away from dying. Their hopes climbed each time Pharaoh agreed to let them go, but then he didn't. They'd viewed Pharaoh's promises as if they were peering out their slavery's open prison door. But in the past each time they gazed toward freedom, the door slammed in their face.

When Moses gave the instructions the first time, no one spoke directly to him. It was late and they couldn't see well, everyone having worked until dusk. A few men in the crowd spoke to one another in response. "Not again." Or, "We've followed them before and it hasn't worked." And, "They've gotten us into more trouble."

A man close to Aaron spoke, "I'm against it. We've been tossed around like rats in a dog's mouth. So far, nothing you've promised has gotten us out of here. Why should we kill one of our best lambs, go through all the fuss with the blood and dinner, and trust that you know what you're talking about?"

Moses knew the people's condition before he and Aaron came to deliver the Lord's message. But Moses continued, believing that in giving them something to do — and not a terribly difficult thing — the Lord was providing them a physical means of bolstering their hope. Moses said, "Do this. It's not much, just a gathering of family and neighbors to eat a lamb whose blood is smeared on the doorposts and lintel of your house."

No one responded this time, just 100 or so dusty men standing hopeless and hungry beyond the sun's last light.

"Just do this," Moses tried one more time. "Get the lamb on the tenth, keep it until the fourteenth, then slaughter it at twilight. Tie up your skirt around your waist, wear your sandals, even in the house, and have your walking staff at hand. This gets you ready to light out to freedom."

"It might get us ready for another beating," a man said. The crowd was growing larger around Moses and Aaron as, in the darkness, more work groups trudged toward their evening meal. As each man arrived he heard the reason for the gathering from the man who arrived before him. The sweat of the day's work hung in the air like the smell of despair. Would these men go home and prepare their families as they were told? Would they carry out Moses' instructions, which sounded so bizarre? Would the Lord this time decisively smash Pharaoh's pride and Pharaoh's people?

Aaron stepped closer to Moses and spoke loudly, "Friends, you've been faithful. You've waited. You've hoped. You've suffered Pharaoh's wrath as he has fruitlessly struggled against the Lord."

"We sure have," a voice came from the men, and many grumbled their agreement.

"But this isn't much to do as you wait and hope one more time," Aaron said. "If *you* can't believe that the Lord will cast a final plague upon the Egyptians, at least take this one step for the rest of us. Don't destroy the faith and hope of the whole Hebrew people.

You can *do* something that might help everyone. Moses and I ask you, for the sake of the faith of all the Hebrew people, do this for them if not for the Lord."

Most of the men turned to leave. Even if they wanted to question or argue more, they didn't have the energy. A few stayed with Moses and Aaron a while longer. "You're just getting us into more trouble," a man said. "Sure are," another agreed.

"Let's give it a try," a third man said. He stood by Moses. "We've had our hopes crushed. We have less food now than before. We almost don't have anything to lose. It's a try. If nothing happens, the Egyptians won't even know we've eaten a meal together. They seldom come around our huts. They won't see the blood on our lintels and doorposts. Let's do it and hope. Moses and Aaron have bloodied their foreheads against Pharaoh for months now. Let's do it for them."

"All right," one man said, as he turned to leave. The Hebrew beside him joined him, but said, "I don't know." The others left, shuffling home to eat, to think, and to tell their wives and children about a special meal that seemed ridiculous but that Moses and Aaron repeatedly begged them to do even if they were out of faith or the hope that the Lord's miracles would free them.

* * *

Later, the Passover meal that the Hebrews prepared was remembered as a night different than all other nights. Later, the ritual feast they ate was repeated and venerated; but, on *this* evening, first hearing of what they were to do, the people were stunned.

At times, our faith is low and our hope hits the minus numbers — like the faith of those Hebrews in the thirteenth century BC. Jesus' disciples experienced such emotions when Jesus was arrested after the Passover meal. However, we, as they — strong or weak in faith, buoyant or sinking in hope — come to the Lord's table as the people who try to obey Jesus when he says merely, "Do this in remembrance of me." Then, on this night with our Hebrew ancestors and with Jesus' faltering disciples, no matter how crushing the circumstance, we wait for the miracles to begin.

Discussion Questions

1. What immediate responses do you have to the story?

2. Do you identify with a character in the story? If yes, how and why do you identify with the person? If no, why don't you identify with anyone in the story?

3. Would you like to have a conversation with a character in the story? What would you say, ask, or suggest to the person? Why?

4. How does the story bring the biblical text into a clearer focus for you?

5. How would you improve or modify the story? Why?

6. Can you put yourself in the Hebrews' place and imagine how they felt and what they thought about the special meal the Lord commanded?

7. When has the Passover meal or the Lord's Supper meant the least to you? When the most?

8. How has your attitude and belief in religious rituals or sacraments changed over the years?

9. What further depths of meaning, symbols, connections with, or applications of the biblical faith do you find in the story?

10. Since Jesus Christ has risen from the dead and is alive among us through his Holy Spirit, what of this story would you like Christ to activate in your life?

Emphasis or special occasion: Grief

Chapter 3

Mid Cemetery

2 Samuel 1:1-17

Gene Marsden remained at the grave until all other mourners were gone. He knew he had to leave. Yet he stayed as the cemetery workers lowered the casket and covered it with dirt. He knew he must go home; but he insisted to the funeral director that he was all right and that he wanted to be here until all was done — canopy removed and the fake grass rolled up and tossed with the folding chairs into the back of the sexton's yellow pickup. He watched until the cemetery workers finished and the new grave lay bumpy under the tired perfume of a few flowers and the re-laid turf.

Staying made him feel no better but at least Gene was safe here from the friends who descended upon him in his grief and who, he was sure, awaited him at a series of well-meaning ambushes. Immediately after Shirley died, he couldn't find the words to say to his friends. By the time he finally formed his thoughts, he didn't have the emotional strength to tell them he didn't want their encouragement. He hurt too much to be consoled. In a seventh grade basketball game someone's elbow landed square on top of his head and gave him a slight concussion. He felt now as if he had a concussion.

He didn't need to hear suggestions that Shirley was in a better place. When Cherie talked to him, he felt like a refrigerator upon which she was attaching a sticky note with a clever saying. He dared not answer after Marty said that God needed Shirley in heaven. If Gene had spoken at that moment, he would have ruined their friendship. He definitely had negative things to say about a God who did such things.

For five days, silently defending himself as best he could, he'd carried on his life by habit and no tears. Habit for five days: Getting up in the morning at the same time, drinking coffee from the same cup, eating the same cereal, and exiting the empty house at 7:20 a.m.

Why not go to work? Nothing at home. Habit guided his Volkswagen to the office, parking in the same spot. Habit got him through the door and to his desk. Then by habit he punched numbers into the telephone and took the orders or answered the questions.

If he were able to speak of his grief, he'd say, "I need to hurt." Nothing too complicated about that, except that he possessed the finest bunch of well-meaning friends that ever burdened a new widower.

He even hesitated now to leave the cemetery, although he'd been here for at least three hours and had begun to walk through the graves, coming back always to stare down at his muddy shoes beside the small, temporary marker: "Shirley Roberts Marsden." He didn't think about what her body looked like now. He kept himself from doing so. He thought of how in the last month he'd often laid awake looking at her dark form in bed and he'd occasionally reached out to touch her face.

He must abandon the cemetery soon, return home, and probably endure an evening of friends systematically checking in on him by phone. They'd hound him the next day by bringing food to his door.

Now his fatigue seemed to leap upon him, and he was so tired he could hardly walk. He turned toward the parking lot and saw, walking toward him, Pastor Mikowski. He couldn't avoid the pastor, nor did he know him well enough to ask to be alone. He was the pastor his friends recommended for the service. Pastor Mik hadn't spoken long at the funeral, but Gene still didn't remember anything he said. Now, he felt defeated, unable even here to escape the do-gooders. He might as well meet Mik and take another verbal beating.

"Hello, Gene," Pastor Mik said.

"Hi."

"Stayed out here a long time, huh?"

"Yeah."

"Hard to leave, isn't it?"

"Uh," Gene said, meaning, "Yes," but unable to say more.

"Everybody's sorry we can't do more for you," Mik said, and then he stood in front of Gene, saying nothing. Two men in suits, standing in the middle of the cemetery, late afternoon, in silence. They stood with slumped shoulders, Gene facing slightly away from the pastor. He thought Mik would say more, but he didn't. Finally, Gene said, "I hurt all over."

Mik nodded his head. They stood there for another five, maybe ten minutes. Gene said, "I miss her everywhere I turn."

Mik leaned closer to Gene and put his hand on his shoulder. Gene was not only exhausted, he was tired of standing in one position, but neither man moved, except for the tiny staccato motions convulsing around Gene's torso, and soon he heard within himself gurgling sounds, almost hiccups. And then he sobbed. Not a tear for five days, but now weeping almost more intensely than he could bear. Mik caught him as his knees gave out, held him tight, and didn't utter a word. Gene Marsden, in his desperation, began the loud part of his grieving in the arms of a man he hardly knew, but whose silence he trusted.

Discussion Questions

1. What immediate responses do you have to the story?

2. Do you identify with a character in the story? If yes, how and why do you identify with the person? If no, why don't you identify with anyone in the story?

3. Would you like to have a conversation with a character in the story? What would you say, ask, or suggest to the person? Why?

4. How does the story bring the biblical text into a clearer focus for you?

5. How would you improve or modify the story? Why?

6. What is your "style" of grieving — with others or alone, speaking or silent?

7. Have you been "hounded by do-gooders" in your suffering or grief?

8. How best have you found to offer your concern to people in grief?

9. What further depths of meaning, symbols, connections with, or applications of the biblical faith do you find in the story?

10. Since Jesus Christ has risen from the dead and is alive among us through his Holy Spirit, what of this story would you like Christ to activate in your life?

Chapter 4

Solomon's Prayer

1 Kings 8:22-30, 42-43

Fifteen years of spaghetti suppers and charity golf tournaments. Fifteen years of scrimping on the present to pay for the future. Some years were stronger than others, with church members whipping up support for the building fund and keeping the goal alive. At other times the project languished, needing another person or group to grab the vision and pull the congregation along. The congregation did it, not the pastors. The decade-and-a-half's saving for the down payment overlapped three pastoral terms. Pastors came and went, but the building project held the congregation together.

Only one pastor contributed to the plans. As ideas for the interior of the building were garnered during the second capital funds drive, her middle school class was studying 1 Kings. From that study, the group suggested to the long-range planning committee that a Bible quote be painted in the large entryway above the doors. No one had thought of such a thing, and when the middle school class suggested a text from Solomon's prayer for the dedication of the temple, people agreed. Few people read the 1 Kings passage; besides, the building was yet a long ways in the future. Their text, with a few words omitted and then the periods signifying the ellipses also omitted, was to be painted ten feet high around the entryway, so you had to spin to read the whole thing: "When a foreigner, who is not of your people, comes and prays toward this house, then hear in heaven, and do according to all that the foreigner calls to you, so that all the peoples of the earth may know your name and fear you" (1 Kings 8:41-43).

By the time the denomination finally granted a loan for the second two-thirds of the total price, everyone's ideas had been pooled into the building design (including the quote from 1 Kings, saved dutifully by three high school students) and the joy of the first shovel turned! Within eight months the congregation moved from their small, downtown building, lacking a parking lot and having too many steps, to their four-acre, one-story campus in the suburbs.

Nineteen months later, a group of Hispanic Christians inquired of each congregation in town, requesting space to rent for worship on Sunday evenings.

The board received the delegation and listened politely, asked a few questions, and would have refused them kindly, if the group hadn't gotten mixed up by the directions the pastor had given over the phone about where to find the board meeting. They came into the building through the main entrance and were overjoyed to read, and report to the board that they'd read, what they assumed was the congregation's mission statement in the large entryway. "When a foreigner, who is not of your people, comes and prays toward this house, then hear in heaven, and do according to all that the foreigner calls to you, so that all the peoples of the earth may know your name and fear you."

When the group departed with many thank yous, the first and principal reason for not renting the church to them was that "sometimes we need the sanctuary on Sunday evenings."

"When?" asked the pastor. This pastor was one year from retirement.

"Sometimes," the board agreed.

"When was the last time? Have we held any Sunday evening events in the sanctuary since we moved into this building?"

No one could remember any. At this juncture someone moved to table the discussion until the next month's meeting, stating the need for prayer over such a matter.

The word zipped through the membership, and few were positive about another group's using their church. Three high school students, however, thought it was what the church was for.

Some members might have prayed about it, but the high school students didn't see much evidence of prayer. The students did, however, quote the Bible text in the entryway a number of times, having memorized its abbreviated form. During prayer concerns, Drusilla, a high school senior, held the microphone with shaking hands. "We need to pray about the Hispanic congregation getting a place to worship." Josh on her one side clenched his fist beside his forehead and Tawn on her other side nodded and said, "Yes!"

After worship the three talked to a board member who said, "I guess we could do it, if we had proper guarantees, liability insurance and all."

When they cornered another board member, she said, "Yes, I've been thinking about it. We all have."

No one in the congregation had been a member of a church that rented its space to another congregation, but one couple had been members of a new congregation that rented space in a school gym until they built a church. The discussion was hot at times. Some people changed their thinking, then changed it back, as ideas both for and against renting passed through the congregation.

Finally, after the issue was tabled two months in a row, the board announced it would vote at Thursday's meeting. The motion to rent, with proper guarantees, liability insurance and all, was made by a member who first quoted Solomon's prayer as it circled their entryway. Another board member said, "Spare the lecture. Let's vote." The board's decision was ...

* * *

What do you think? Raise your hand if you think they voted yes. How many of you think they voted no? When Jesus told such stories he often ended with something like, "Go and do likewise." How would *you* vote, believing as did Solomon when he prayed for the temple, "Even heaven and the highest heaven cannot contain you, much less this house that I have built!"

Discussion Questions

1. What immediate responses do you have to the story?

2. Do you identify with a character in the story? If yes, how and why do you identify with the person? If no, why don't you identify with anyone in the story?

3. Would you like to have a conversation with a character in the story? What would you say, ask, or suggest to the person? Why?

4. How does the story bring the biblical text into a clearer focus for you?

5. How would you improve or modify the story? Why?

6. Have you been in a congregation that argued over the use of its church building(s)?

7. What's the best design idea you've seen that contributes to a full and varied use of a church building?

8. If you were to design a building that would serve Christ in many ways, how would you design it and for what other than worship would it serve?

9. What further depths of meaning, symbols, connections with, or applications of the biblical faith do you find in the story?

10. Since Jesus Christ has risen from the dead and is alive among us through his Holy Spirit, what of this story would you like Christ to activate in your life?

Chapter 5

Unanswerable

Job 38:1-7

"Why do some apples have scabs on them?" Kevin looked up to his sister.

"If they're all perfect," Allison answered, "you wouldn't have a special one to look forward to." The two young children stood in the evening sunset. The clouds still covered most of the sky. Water dripped from the five fruit trees beside their house.

"Why did it rain today," he asked, "when we were going to have a picnic?"

"Well," Allison said, "we didn't need to go to the park today. We can go tomorrow."

"I still wish we could've gone today," Kevin said.

Allison gave him a knowing smile. Kevin wasn't satisfied, but Allison seemed to be. She kicked the wet grass as they walked. She shuffled, humming, clearly pleased to have a younger brother for whom she could provide such obvious answers. As they walked up the front steps to their home, Allison said confidently, "You'll understand more when you're old enough to go to Sunday school."

Five years later, when Kevin was ten and Allison was twelve, Kevin asked, "How come I struck out tonight with the bases loaded?"

"You tried your best," she said, pursing her lips and wrinkling her forehead, "Maybe you struck out so you'll want to take extra batting practice and get better."

"I will," he said as they walked slowly up the sidewalk to their home. "But why did Josh have to yell at me that I was stupid and I'd lost the game for the whole team?"

"I guess," Allison sighed, "because he's never been taught manners, or he's never struck out."

"He's really good. Never strikes out. But I already felt bad enough. What'll I do if he yells at me every time I make a mistake?"

"Just keep trying." Allison patted him on the back as he opened the door. Their father was talking on the phone. He covered the receiver and pointed to the kitchen, "Your mom's got supper for you."

When Kevin was sixteen and Allison was eighteen, she opened his bedroom door slowly. Kevin sat on the floor, back to his bed, rhythmically pounding his left fist onto the carpet. He looked up at her through red eyes. He kept banging his fist onto the floor. "Why did he have to die? Everyone else walked away." He shut his eyes tightly and tipped his head back against his bed. The veins on his neck bulged as he started to cry again.

"He was unlucky. But they *were* speeding. The police said ninety miles an hour."

"But why Mark? Why Mark? Pete's such an idiot and he's the one driving. Mark's the best guy in the world. Why Mark?"

Allison bent over Kevin. "Whoever sat in the passenger's seat would've been killed."

By Christmas of Kevin's first year of graduate school, Allison had been married to Stuart for three years. Their son, also named Kevin, was two and their daughter, Mamie, was three months old. Because Allison and Stuart lived far way, this was the first Christmas gathering for the family since Allison and Stuart had married. Kevin brought his girlfriend, Daphne, home for Christmas, too.

The grandparents gladly took care of the children and the four "young people," as the grandparents called them, enjoyed two days together. The first day included a morning at the skating rink that resulted in Daphne spraining her wrist. Another day at the mall left them all tired.

On Christmas morning after the presents were opened, Kevin handed an envelope to his parents and one to Allison and Stuart. "Open them at the same time," he said. He and Daphne sat on the couch, holding hands and smiling. Allison let Stuart open their envelope. She dandled Mamie on her leg and leaned toward her brother and his girlfriend. She smirked knowingly at them.

The envelope held this announcement: "This is to announce that Daphne Ann Sperry will become the wife of Kevin George Boren. Date to be determined."

"You came through in the clutch," his father said and shook Kevin's hand. Allison was squeezing Daphne, who held her injured hand above the hug. Their mother got her chance to hug Daphne and said, "I let my son choose my second daughter and he's done very well."

For Christmas dinner, Kevin and Allison assumed their childhood chore of bringing all the food from the kitchen to the dining room. They piled bowls, plates, and gravy boats onto trays in the kitchen. With the flourish of a bullfighter, Kevin bumped his hip against his sister's. "So, tell me, big sis, why do you suppose Daphne wants to marry me?"

Allison held the platter of turkey in front of her, bending slightly as she stepped backward, pushing open the swinging door behind her, and said, "I haven't got the slightest idea."

Discussion Questions

1. What immediate responses do you have to the story?

2. Do you identify with a character in the story? If yes, how and why do you identify with the person? If no, why don't you identify with anyone in the story?

3. Would you like to have a conversation with a character in the story? What would you say, ask, or suggest to the person? Why?

4. How does the story bring the biblical text into a clearer focus for you?

5. How would you improve or modify the story? Why?

6. Why do humans so often look for reasons to explain the world's bad or good happenings?

7. Has someone confidently told you the reasons for good or bad things happening to you?

8. As a Christian what are the most helpful things to say or do when a suffering person asks why tragedies occur?

9. What further depths of meaning, symbols, connections with, or applications of the biblical faith do you find in the story?

10. Since Jesus Christ has risen from the dead and is alive among us through his Holy Spirit, what of this story would you like Christ to activate in your life?

Emphasis or special occasion: Christmas Eve

Chapter 6

O People Walking In Darkness

Isaiah 9:2

> *O people walking in darkness, behold a great light. You who are dwelling in the region and shadow of death, a light will shine upon you.* — Isaiah 9:2

Note: This is the author's translation of the Greek translation of the Hebrew Old Testament. The Greek translation became the "Christian" Old Testament for centuries. The Greek translation was begun in Alexandria, Egypt, in the third century BC and is commonly named the Septuagint.

* * *

Mitch Larkin held aside the drapes and peered out the window into the evening's snow. Darkness piling up by the inch. Made no difference that snow was white. It was dark — seemed as though it had always been dark. Yet, he'd do as he promised. He sighed, turned from the window, and again stared at the Larkin family photograph, faint in the light of one lamp. He'd taken the portrait with him when he moved out and kept it when the rest of the family moved away: ex-wife, Jane; daughter, Stephanie; son, Theodore.

Alone on Christmas Eve, he shuffled from the window to the kitchen table. Nothing wrong, physically, just the darkness outside and within. He moved haltingly because what he planned to do this night might be the hardest thing he'd done for half his life. He first fortified himself with a cup of instant coffee, super-black, then struggled through a shower and shave and put on his suit with the effort of preparing to attend a funeral.

Mitch had been, as he euphemistically put it, interested in other women. No reason to hide it now. No use making it sound as though he merely did as everyone else was doing. No blaming Jane or claiming that a high-stress job pushed him to it. It was his fault, he knew. He told himself 947, 948, 949 times. Quietly, in the living room's shadows, he spoke to himself or to the universe. It made no difference, the words landed upon the evening's dim emptiness: "Mitch Larkin was wrong."

At seventy, he no longer chased women, whether single or married. He survived adequately. The divorce settlement left him three-fourths of his pension, then Social Security, some savings. He drove a five-year-old car. Not a bad house. All paid for, all his, whether on Christmas Eve or any other night or day, each seeming to pile up deeper layers of darkness.

Mitch didn't like driving after dark anymore, but he must force himself to keep his word. He closed the front door behind him, feeling the stab of the cold night. The television predicted fifteen below tonight. He began the labor of brushing snow from his car.

Earlier that day, at eight-fifteen in the morning, the telephone had rung. "Hello, Dad?"

"Yeah?"

"Dad, it's Ted." Ted telephoned once a month.

"Oh. Hi, uh, Son. Merry Christmas," was all Mitch could say.

"Merry Christmas, Dad."

Then a brief silence between them, a distant, lonely silence. Mitch managed, "How are Jessica and the kids?"

"Fine, they're just great. Everything's hectic this week. Earl sang at concerts Tuesday and Wednesday nights. Diana got home from college Thursday."

"What you doing for Christmas?"

"We'll be at Mom's with Steph and Jack."

"Oh." He winced. "Well, tell everyone 'Hello' for me."

Another silence. Mitch stared out the window at the morning's snow without a blink or smile.

"Dad?"

"Uh huh."

"Dad, I ... I'd like you to do something for me and Jess."

"Do something?"

"Jess and I've been talking. Are you going anywhere tonight?"

"Tonight? Well, no. Why?"

"We'd like you to do something for us."

As though he were in business again, Mitch changed the receiver to his left hand and reached for the pencil by the phone. He leaned down toward the tablet upon the telephone table. "Okay, what is it?"

"We'd like you to go to worship tonight, like when Steph and I were kids. We'd drive if we were there, but three states away makes it kind of tough." He uttered a fast laugh. "And Christmas has got to be lonely for you."

"No," Mitch said instantly. "I'm not lonely."

"Good. But would you go to worship tonight?"

Mitch let out his breath, but made sure it wasn't heard in the receiver. He looked at the family portrait again, taken for the church directory 26 years before. He needed to answer quickly so that Ted wouldn't recognize his reluctance.

"Sure, Son. I'll go to church tonight."

"Promise?"

"Of course, I promise."

"Great, Dad. We're glad to hear that. Even from quarter of a continent away that's good news."

Again a pause. Ted obviously had no more to say. Mitch had nothing he was willing to say, except perhaps that Ted was awfully cute in the family portrait: curly black hair, green blazer.

"Wonderful," Ted said. "Well, Merry Christmas, Dad."

"Yes, Merry Christmas, son."

Mitch would keep his word no matter the cold, the snow, or the dark. His right shoulder was aching by the time he removed the snow from the car windows, now revealing ice to scrape. He had lived his years of deception, his intricate lies, all bent and tangled and sometimes so complicated they were hard to remember. He put together alibis and created more excuses than McDonald's cooked hamburgers. Over the last months, out of nowhere, the words slipped from him: "I was wrong."

The snowing stopped, which would make driving easier. He took a last, deep breath, sucking in the cold, and, with a thump, planted himself in the driver's seat.

"Church" meant Trinity Presbyterian and he found the building standing as if it had had nothing to do for a quarter of a century except wait for those who finally returned for, well, Christmas Eve worship. He parked and sat quietly in the car for half a minute, then firmly gripped the steering wheel, gritted his teeth, and said, "I *will* go in there."

He knocked snow off his shoes before he walked into the well-lit sanctuary. It was painted a different color and the chancel was rearranged, but otherwise it was pretty much as he remembered. He saw three people he knew. By waving and continuing to walk, he didn't have to talk to them. He hadn't been a regular attendee, and although he felt uneasy, the place was familiar.

He had been sitting about four minutes when the acolytes entered with the candlelighters, then the organ swelled and the pastor led the choir down the aisle as all stood to sing: "Joy To The World." He'd endure the service. He promised he would. This time he was going to tell the truth as well as do what he said he'd do.

The singing was pleasant and the organ shook the building, seeming to vibrate the walls. The choir sang an anthem, college students read the Christmas story from the gospels, prayer was offered. But it was the Bible passage before the message that caught Mitch's interest.

The pastor said, "The text this evening is Isaiah, chapter 9, verse 2. I will read an English translation of a Greek translation, old even before Jesus was born. It states, 'O people walking in darkness, behold a great light. You who are dwelling in the region and shadow of death, a light will shine upon you.' " The pastor placed the Bible to the side, saying, "God blesses those who hear scripture as God's word to them."

He hesitated, looking down at the pulpit. Mitch gazed at the candles in the chancel that splattered their orange light throughout the building.

"On this Christmas Eve, God speaks to each of us from the scripture. God addresses us personally, 'O people walking in darkness.' To all of us in darkness God promises a great light. God's light will shine in our darkness, the darkness over or under us, between us, outside or inside us. The promise is from God who cannot lie. The promise: 'You who are dwelling in the region and shadow of death, a light will shine upon you.' The light comes in an extraordinary — in fact, a unique — person: Jesus the promised Christ who brings true peace.

"There are a multitude of things that could be said about Christmas, and a myriad of ways to say them. For now, if you take anything from this worship, make it this."

Make it this? Mitch thought. But the pastor had merely paused longer than usual.

"Make it this: No matter how dark our lives, world, or relationships, no matter how dark our neighborhood, church, or nation, no matter how dark our prospects for tomorrow or our sins from yesterday, God makes this promise — a symbol, of course, as so much of the Bible is symbols and we are to figure them out and apply them, but this: 'You who are dwelling in the region and shadow of death, a light will shine upon you.' That was the good news Isaiah pronounced centuries before Jesus' birth, the good news that finally led over the years even through different Bible translations to fulfillment in Jesus, and the good news that tonight, through Jesus, shines for all people. You might see that light ever so dimly; but the promise of light, God's promise of light, still comes to 'You who are dwelling in the region and shadow of death.' "

Mitch looked intently upon the center candle encircled by the Advent wreath. As he stood to leave he noticed that the center candle was white, with a cross upon it.

"Hi, Mitch." A church member shook his hand as he stepped out of his seat.

"Hello, Tom," he said.

"Glad to see you," Tom said. "What brought you out tonight?"

"Thank you," Mitch said with a polite smile. "I'm glad I came."

Mitch meant what he said, but he didn't want to talk to anyone right now. He left the building quickly so that outside he could finally say to himself and to the universe what he couldn't complete to Tom Macmillan, "I had to come because of a promise."

As he walked to his car, he noticed that through the stained-glass windows, the sanctuary lights cast all the rainbow's colors onto the snow.

Discussion Questions

1. What immediate responses do you have to the story?

2. Do you identify with a character in the story? If yes, how and why do you identify with the person? If no, why don't you identify with anyone in the story?

3. Would you like to have a conversation with a character in the story? What would you say, ask, or suggest to the person? Why?

4. How does the story bring the biblical text into a clearer focus for you?

5. How would you improve or modify the story? Why?

6. How do you celebrate Christmas Eve and Christmas Day? What are your most meaningful memories of family and Christmas?

7. How has the Christmas season helped or hurt your faith?

8. Have you experienced God's speaking directly to you during a worship service? Has this happened at Christmas?

9. What further depths of meaning, symbols, connections with, or applications of the biblical faith do you find in the story?

10. Since Jesus Christ has risen from the dead and is alive among us through his Holy Spirit, what of this story would you like Christ to activate in your life?

Emphasis or special occasion: Baccalaureate or Graduation

Chapter 7

The Twins

Hosea 11:3

Note for reading aloud: A good deal of the dialogue is not tagged with "he said," "she said." However, when reading aloud, merely speak Tom's voice lower and Trina's higher. The end of the story includes an option actually used at a baccalaureate service, having listeners repeat a blessing after the reader. The ages and dates may be changed to make the story more relevant.

* * *

Graduates, parents and family, friends and neighbors, faculty and administration: The message tonight is a story, following the pattern of Jesus who told stories to dramatize the way God works in the world. The story's title is "The Twins."

The twins, Tom and Trina, were born February 17, 1984. So, graduates, they are your contemporaries. They, too, will graduate in the class of 2002.

Tom and Trina fought a lot when they were younger. As children, they competed against one another to win the many games they created or to get the better grades. In the last few years, they've bickered over who got the car on Friday and Saturday nights. After New Year's Day 2002, however, they began being nicer to one another. Neither has said so, but they each feel strange, considering that come fall they'll attend different colleges. They'll be apart for the first time in their lives.

The twins have much in common besides their parents and birth date. One thing: Neither of them has liked church much. They haven't actively *dis*liked it. The message has just never seemed intended for them. As children, about all they did in worship was try to catch their parents not looking so they could pinch each other.

This past Sunday, something began to make sense for them. Tom picked it up first, although not immediately. They attended church with their parents and, although it's been a long time since they played their Sunday morning pinching game, still neither considered worship captivating. The pastor spoke about God's loving everyone from childhood and Tom, especially, was fascinated by the Bible's message that God had taught Israel to walk. He didn't understand fully, nor did he much care, that the Bible *says* God teaches a child to walk and *means* that God instructs an entire nation how to live.

When they arrived home from church, they left their parents in the kitchen. Tom was following Trina. He said, "Did you picture God helping a little kid walk?"

"No, not really," Trina turned around as they walked upstairs. "Obviously you did."

"Yeah, that was kind of awesome. Makes God seem a lot more human."

"You got that mixed up," Trina said. "Pretty tough to be God and human at the same time."

Upstairs, they slumped onto the sofa. "Well, maybe not exactly human," Tom said, "but I could just see God bending down helping a kid take its first steps like the picture Mom shows everybody of Grandma holding you up and Grandpa holding me up as we learned to walk."

"You were crying," Trina said.

Tom faked a kick at her. She flinched.

"Okay, okay, I see what you mean," Trina said. "I like the idea. If God's like that, it doesn't sound so bad."

They turned on the television to a *Get Smart* rerun. After seven minutes, Trina picked up the remote and switched it off. She could tell that Tom was thinking the same things she was. She didn't have to explain, just started talking. "It means that God was around when we took *our* first steps."

"And when we fell on our faces," Tom said.

"I wonder if God liked seeing us learn to talk, or twirl, or ride a bike? Suppose God watched our first soccer game?"

"Probably laughed," Tom said, "at you, anyway."

Trina slugged him, but not hard. They sat silently. They heard their mother downstairs in the kitchen shut the refrigerator and put a pan on the stove, starting lunch.

"The Bible quoted God as saying, 'I taught Ephraim to walk,' " Trina said. "I do like that."

"So, God saw us when we first stubbed our toes or sprained our ankles," Tom said and he tipped up the end of his sentence, which signaled Trina that it was her turn. Trina caught it instantly. "When we lost our first teeth," She said.

"And got our braces," Tom said.

They were off, bantering back and forth faster than they volleyed in tennis, playing the game they'd perfected over years — seeing which, in turn, could say the most about a subject.

"God watched us fighting over My Little Ponies," Trina said.

"And saw you get cotton candy in your hair at the circus."

"God saw you win the school's foursquare championship."

"God saw you draw the first picture that actually looked like the person you intended."

"God saw the bus drive over your lunch bucket."

"Saw you cry," he said slowly, "when you lost your fuzzy, pink coat."

"God watched you get stitches on your chin."

"And God was there when you had the crush on Mr. Coats."

"And when you woke every night for a month with the same nightmare."

"When you started wearing a bra."

"Ha," she slapped him and said with a lilt, "when your voice changed."

"And," Tom said, "maybe God knew what we felt when we left grade school for junior high."

"And knew what it was like for us to enter high school."

"And learn to drive."

"And dent the fender."

"God saw you pierce your nose."

"And dye your hair purple."

"And was there when your best friend, Carrie, moved away."

"When you missed the foul shots that lost the game against Central."

"Then," he hesitated, "then, maybe God knew what it was like for us when Grandpa died."

They paused. Each could tell what the other was thinking. Quietly, Trina said, "God also must have known when you lied to Dad and went to the drinking party at the old mill."

"And when I dared you to shoplift from K-mart."

"But, but," Trina said, "God must know that we admitted what we did was wrong and that we went back and paid for what I took."

"Then ... ah ..." Tom said.

"What?" she said.

"I don't know," he said. "Now that I think about it, I'm not sure I like God knowing all those things."

They each had thought of enough items to play until midnight, but the game was over. They smelled hamburgers frying, but neither felt very hungry.

Tom and Trina. Your age. Ready to graduate. Worrying about the future. Realizing that God knows all they've done. Wondering what God might think of them.

A lot of people worry that God sees and remembers the bad things they've done, which is true. God knows all we've thought and said, the mistakes we've made, the people we've hurt; but, God knows so much more. God knows our most painful regrets and worries, our highest aspirations, our hopes to be better people, and our deepest desires for faith. God knows us through and through, and God doesn't love us less for knowing us best.

In the Old Testament, Hosea chapter 11, the prophet speaks of God's tender concern for us by saying, "I taught Ephraim [meaning the Hebrew people] to walk." Graduates: God has created you and planned that you walk and run, grow and mature. God has cared for you as children and enjoyed seeing you advance toward adulthood. God never quits loving us. We're always important to God, valuable to God, beloved to God — no matter how old we are.

There's more to know about God, including how he *could* become human. For now, one thing to remember, and it's wonderful news for people of all ages: God knows you better even than does your twin, better than you know yourself, and he loves you, anyway.

God knows you the best and loves you the most. That's the Bible's message that each of us needs to learn first and remember always.

Whether you've heard the good news of God's love every Sunday and believed it all your life, or if you've never really understood how God could know and love each of us, graduation is an occasion that summons all of us to grasp the center of the Christian faith and hold on for life.

Whether you feel confident in your Christian faith or if you're not certain at all about God, please join in speaking and hearing the good news for Tom and Trina and for God's children of all ages. If we repeat it together, we'll remember it longer. As our way of blessing the graduates together, would everyone please repeat after me:

> *God, who knows you ...*
> *God, who knows you best, loves you ...*
> *loves you ...*
> *God, who knows you best, loves you the most....*
> *Amen.*

Discussion Questions

1. What immediate responses do you have to the story?

2. Do you identify with a character in the story? If yes, how and why do you identify with the person? If no, why don't you identify with anyone in the story?

3. Would you like to have a conversation with a character in the story? What would you say, ask, or suggest to the person? Why?

4. How does the story bring the biblical text into a clearer focus for you?

5. How would you improve or modify the story? Why?

6. What do you remember of your high school graduation or baccalaureate, or that of your children's or of other significant people?

7. Did you have a time of wondering if God's knowing everything about you disqualified you from God's love?

8. If you had the privilege of speaking to high school graduates, what would you tell them that they most need to hear about God and how would you tell them so it would make sense to them?

9. What further depths of meaning, symbols, connections with, or applications of the biblical faith do you find in the story?

10. Since Jesus Christ has risen from the dead and is alive among us through his Holy Spirit, what of this story would you like Christ to activate in your life?

Emphasis or special occasion: Epiphany

Chapter 8

The Chief Magi's Son

Matthew 2:1-12

The chief magi's son had never wanted to leave Persia and go off after a star; during the weeks on the journey, if anyone would listen to him, he tried to make them understand: "Stars shine everywhere." His magi companions habitually smiled at his contrariness. His father, the chief magi, endured his questions even when they bordered more on blasphemy than interrogation: "Look at the sky. Has it changed since we left three months ago?" His father, no matter how difficult the road or how hot the day, said, "You'll see." When that response didn't convince his son, the chief magi smiled and patted him on the shoulder.

Now they'd gone through the mockery of an interview with Herod. The chief magi's son felt the hair on his neck prickle when Herod displayed his oily smile. Did they really think this tyrant was pleased that a rival king was born outside his dynastic line? As they were escorted from Herod's audience room he whispered to two magi, "Don't you see that Herod is suspicious?" But, since he had been such a consistent nag for months, the magi smiled gently and made their preparations to continue toward Bethlehem. Truly, the chief magi's son didn't try as hard to convince them anymore. No matter their expectations for his also becoming a magi, he only came along because he promised his mother to watch out for his father. The magis' infinite patience with him had worn him down.

Only once more did he try to convince his father that they were putting their heads in the lion's mouth. His father replied, "Yes, the lion of the tribe of Judah." His father shushed him, "We're almost there." He patted his son on the shoulder. "Another morning's travel. You'll see."

The next morning they left Jerusalem — camels, donkeys, attendants, and magi. The chief magi's son made sure he was last. He glanced back toward Jerusalem and saw Herod's men atop the city wall, watching them. He expected to see them again soon.

What had captured the minds of these Zoroastrian priests who, until a year ago, had seemed so reasonable, so stable, even staid? The dangerous pilgrimage to Judea was only one thing. To think that a star could guide them anywhere was foolish and bordered on self-destruction. Didn't they realize you can see a star from anywhere? That's one large sky up there, seen from all points on earth. Stars don't stand over anything. Stars move all night and all year.

The caravan arrived in Bethlehem at midday. Their entourage with their foreign clothes and strange dialect upset the villagers. The magi announced that they came seeking the child born king of the Jews, the Messiah. The chief magi's son sighed and said to a boy holding a camel's bridle, "Why don't we just return to Jerusalem and turn ourselves in for sedition?" Herod would act swiftly if even one village sprouted hope for a different king.

No one in Bethlehem knew of a special baby, although the magi made a number of young mothers happy by their visits. In the late afternoon, the magi gathered for a council and determined they must wait for nightfall and the star to direct them. The chief magi's son sat beyond their circle and remained silent during the discussion.

That evening as the stars appeared, the old men, professional astrologers, stood gazing at the heavens, identifying constellations. One said, "There it is." The others shouted agreement. Then they ran, grabbing the gifts they had carted for 100 days. Adorned in their priestly Persian garb, the old men tottered through the dark street like frail birds flying at night. The chief magi's son followed in order to pick up any who fell. He didn't want them hurt. Who else would have put up with him as they did? He was already planning a way home for them by some route other than through Herod's Jerusalem.

Ahead of him, his father kept looking up at the stars, then down to the dark, irregular alley. He stopped and pointed to the house that he said the star shined over. His son looked up also, seeing all stars shining over all houses. The men knocked and were welcomed in. They entered in such joy they didn't realize that the chief magi's son stayed outside.

He had kept his father safe halfway. He also promised his mother to usher him home safely. Alone in Bethlehem's dark street, away from the old men's excitement, the chief magi's son looked up quietly and said, "God, I don't know whose child they've come upon. But they're good men full of hopes. They're old men consumed with dreams. They're not like so many people hollowed out by life. These men, led by my father, are looking for something extraordinary. Not for their own benefit. They aren't seeking in order to become rich and powerful.

"Great creator, if you reward anyone for faithfulness, look upon them, I pray. They follow their abnormal star, which they think shines only here. Grant them some touch upon this earth of life beyond. Don't let their waning years be filled with regret. Bestow upon them, I pray, satisfaction with a quest that grows in mercy and kindness and that spreads to others as goodwill.

"Merciful and almighty, if I also must become a priest, I ask that you impart to me a portion of their faith and compassion, for these are the best men I've ever known. And if I, as they expect, must serve an earthly Messiah, may he be as hopeful as these magi and as good as my father.

"In hope for the world I pray. Amen."

Discussion Questions

1. What immediate responses do you have to the story?

2. Do you identify with a character in the story? If yes, how and why do you identify with the person? If no, why don't you identify with anyone in the story?

3. Would you like to have a conversation with a character in the story? What would you say, ask, or suggest to the person? Why?

4. How does the story bring the biblical text into a clearer focus for you?

5. How would you improve or modify the story? Why?

6. Have you considered yourself upon a religious quest? How? What have you sought? What did you find?

7. How has your faith been affected by the people of your parents' age?

8. How do you respond to religious idealists? To religious skeptics?

9. What further depths of meaning, symbols, connections with, or applications of the biblical faith do you find in the story?

10. Since Jesus Christ has risen from the dead and is alive among us through his Holy Spirit, what of this story would you like Christ to activate in your life?

Emphasis or special occasion: Independence Day

Chapter 9
July Fifth

Matthew 5:38-39

Denton called me to his office. He was the obsessive type, viciously tidy, everything carefully in files. I sat on the corner of his desk. "What's up?"

He pointed. "Sit down."

"Sure." I pushed two chairs together. Sat on one. Propped my feet on the other.

"Keith, in the last month you have, at last count, miss-posted three documents at the courthouse. The escrow manager has taken heat from loan departments at two banks. I have," he rattled papers at me, "clients' letters of complaint, and your secretary said she would quit if she has to keep covering for you."

Denton had threatened me before, but arguing with him was so easy. It was almost like play. "Well, I was looking for a job when I found this one."

Denton seemed to leap and landed with his face three inches from mine, "Stop kidding yourself. I *gave* you a job after you begged me as your friend. You hadn't worked well before and for months you haven't done your job well here. You've been drinking too much and thinking too little."

I countered with a sneer. "What are you talking about?" He's a short guy who occasionally tries to make up for his size by not backing down.

"I don't know another forty-year-old who has messed up his job and life worse than you."

"Well, I might have made a couple mistakes lately, but I *am* your best title manager."

"You *are* the occidental end of an orientally directed equine."

I didn't know exactly what that meant, but I caught the drift.

"I shouldn't have given you a job in the first place." He almost slobbered on me. "And everyone tells me I'm asking to be slapped in the face, but I've got too much invested in your training. I'm granting you another chance. Are you listening?"

I looked away from the window and into his squinty, little eyes. "Of course."

"I'll send you to Idaho for three weeks. My favorite village, quiet, surrounded by nature's beauties. I'll put three books in your hand. You have 21 days to read them and get your life together or by autumn you'll be collecting unemployment."

Openings for title managers aren't easy to find right now, even when you're as good as I am. I remained silent.

"Speak back to me the terms."

"You want me to leave for three weeks."

"No, you have the *choice* to leave for three weeks. And if you come back to work, you bring a total attitude change — get along with your coworkers, do accurate and complete work, be courteous to clients — or you're fired. Repeat the terms."

"I'll come back and do a splendid job for all involved."

He continued his repeat-after-me mode. "Leave tomorrow or think about it two days without pay."

"Leave tomorrow," I said, chopping my words sing-songy and precise, "or think about it two days without pay."

He thrust three books at me. "Take these and learn something. And," he jabbed his fingers into my stomach, "get some exercise. Your gut slips all the way over your belt."

I stood erect, saluted, and left. Because of Denton's unreasonable demands, the next morning at 5:30 I was on the freeway traveling east from Portland for three weeks of enforced vacation. Driving into the rising sun blinded me, but I thought of Denton's smug little face and consoled myself that I was spending his money.

I grabbed in the seat beside me: a book about successful people. I tossed it. Another about excellence in human relations. I flipped it. On the bottom, a New Testament. Denton also made me take my laptop to send email updates. I can do this. I'll send chatty observations of Idaho's weather and rave about the books as though I'm undergoing a miracle of self-therapy. I'll make him pay for every minute of those 21 days, then laugh in his face and quit.

Late that afternoon I was roaring into dark clouds, ascending to a pass at 7,000 feet. The gravel road resembled the surface of the moon. I had reached McMahan — the last outpost of civilization — but needed to get to Darrien by evening or pay for a motel. I endured a few squalls, and then the sky emptied upon me for half an hour. I rounded a corner and a wave of water hit, transforming the ditches into riparian zones. No time to turn around. I dented the floorboard with the brake pedal, shifted into park, and managed to crawl through the window onto the roof, ripping my pants and losing a shoe. This is exactly where Denton — not to mention my ex-wife — wants me. If this is Idaho's worst, I can take it.

The brown, rushing water, like life's happiest occasions, rose and fell within a minute and was gone, with a trickling of mud as the only evidence that anything had gone wrong. The car's front was sitting high enough that the water hadn't reached the electrical system. The rear slumped in one of the road's mini-craters, and I knew my trunk was soaked. I dismounted and hobbled on one muddy shoe and one sock. Downstream, my left Nike would someday contribute to Idaho's soil.

In order to make Denton pay for every night's lodging, I raced uphill again, my heater on and my windows half down, trying to dry the car. I had slowed to 55 when I heard the oddest sound, like a train, directly on my left. I looked up. A dozen elk tumbled down the steep cut of the road. They couldn't have fallen more directly onto me if they'd parachuted. One big cow spotted me half a second after I saw her. Her brown eyes looked as large as teacups as her momentum crashed her knees into my driver's door and her head over the top. My side window broke, and her fur, blood, and seven million bits of glass splattered me. She bounced off like a gymnast. The car skipped a foot to the right. I got out to examine the car's mashed-in, bloody, muddy side and shook glass from my clothing. I looked in the direction she ran and raised my fist, "Come back and try again. You didn't get me."

After eight o'clock, I arrived at a hamlet of about 35 unpainted buildings, most of which looked abandoned. The street was empty.

I felt like a gunslinger riding into Dodge City. Two or three cars were parked at houses that didn't look more or less occupied than any other. At the end of the street sat the only two-story structure in the ramshackle group. The hand-lettered sign over the stoop read "Darrien Hotel." It was the end of the trail and the end of the world.

I parked beside a pickup whose tires were taller than my car. I limped to the trunk. As I lifted my dripping gear, a man stepped from the hotel. He was medium height. Gray hair sprouted from under a cap and surrounded his pudgy face, making him look like a Pekingese wearing a hat. He slowly approached, observing the car's mud line, its dislocated left side, the furry bloodstains. He looked at me, wet and dirty, my pants ripped, and his gaze descended to my muddy sock.

"By gum, looks like you had a little trouble. I'm Elmer. Welcome to Darrien." I freed several fingers from my suitcase handle to shake his hand. If I wasn't yet in the twilight zone, he could direct me there.

The sun was almost down when I plopped my dripping luggage in front of the hotel's main desk. It was a cabinet yanked from someone's kitchen, not even repainted. The room's ceiling was irregular of color and patched — a couple places looking as though chamber pots had spilled upstairs. The floor was a miniature of the rolling, brown hills I drove through earlier in the day. No use asking for room service.

I didn't feel happily greeted by my room, although someone once might have been cheered by the place — perhaps Meriwether Lewis. But I wouldn't let a room ruin my appetite. I'd hardly eaten since I bought a map in Pendleton. I'd earned dinner. Actually, I didn't anticipate food so much as beer.

The restaurant consisted of seven tables to the right of the hotel's converted kitchen cabinet. The waiter shuffled over. He was a nondescript young fellow. I ordered two Coors and began to unwind from the trek. After forty minutes of brooding over what Denton had gotten me into, I beckoned the waiter. "Another Coors."

"I'm sorry, sir," he said in a monotone. "Two's the limit."

"I'm considering your special. Bring me another beer and I'll stick my head into this menu and be ready when you get back."

"Sorry, sir. House policy's two drinks in two hours. Nothing I can do, unless you wait another hour."

"That's crazy." I stood up so he wouldn't be looking down on me. "I've never heard of such a thing."

"It's the policy, sir, made because of unhappy experiences." The words sounded like a script. I'd rather he frowned or threatened me or something.

"Unhappy?"

"Violent," he said.

"Well, I'm not violent," I shouted. "I'm a professional."

He didn't wince.

"Listen." I leaned toward him and whispered, smiling, "I've had a terrible day. I'll order now, okay?" I handed him a $5 bill and grabbed the menu.

"That's fine, sir." He laid the money on the table. "But no more alcohol for an hour."

I raised my voice again, "You're supposed to serve me."

"I just did, sir."

Something superior in his manner reminded me of Denton. I slapped the menu on the table, grabbed the $5 back, and walked out. I was disappointed, but not thoroughly miserable. I'd gotten a couple beers. I'd go to the grocery store and buy something. For sure they'd have tiny doughnuts, preserved with waxy frosting and baked before the Apollo moon shots. I walked 100 yards — no store. I replayed my memory tapes of walking into the hotel. Seems there were a couple shelves to the left with groceries. I wouldn't give the waiter the satisfaction of seeing me buy groceries. I opened the car's trunk, grabbed a handful of soggy potato chips and can't say I enjoyed my first evening in Darrien, Idaho.

> *Email. Thursday, June 20, 9:30 p.m.*
> *Dirty Dent,*
> *Automobile nearly shipwrecked in transit, then maimed by wild animal stampede. I sustained major injuries and significant personal losses. Yet sailed safely, if crippled, into port of Darrien, Idaho. With failing strength, checked into your favorite hotel and made*

> *acquaintance with the most obtuse waiter in the three northwestern states.*

In the morning I rose early. I was hungry and too cold to sleep. Since last night took a dozen dialings to get my computer online, I took my cell phone outside and tried to phone my girlfriend. I was examining my phone's display when Elmer walked out.

"By gum, you must've just found out cell phones don't work here."

"Yeah." I jammed it into my pocket.

"But we've got real phones. Lines've been in three years."

"Electricity's irregular." In the night I'd tried the switch in the bathroom.

"Hear that?" It sounded like a truck idling a couple blocks away. "That's the generator: on at 5:30 a.m., off at 11 p.m. That's why the flashlight's next to your bed."

I passed my first day walking around the settlement to determine which houses were the ghost and which were the town. I saw last night's waiter but avoided him, though he didn't seem bright enough to hold a grudge. The second night I found the flashlight.

> *Email. Saturday, June 22.*
> *Major Dent,*
> > *Reporting as ordered. Have discovered Idaho's gene pool, and it is shallow, indeed.*

By the third morning, I'd made a chair on the hotel porch my post. I crossed my arms to endure three weeks while I added up all Denton's insults and contemplated ways to burn down the title company — after Denton paid my car repairs.

> *Email. Wednesday, June 26*
> *Dent,*
> > *Did you know the hotel is a multipurpose business? Old geezer here who encourages me to buy gum says Christmas Eve and Easter morning it's a church.*

On the sixth day, I began reading the hotel's old magazines, tiring myself so much that in the afternoon I began to catch up on the last four years of sleep. On the seventh day, I formulated an ingenious plan to corrupt Denton's computer files.

> *Email. Saturday, June 29, 10 p.m.*
> Dent,
> This morning, horseback riding with all the Boy Scouts in the state. Afternoon, water polo with the Olympic team. After dinner at the club, a leisurely game of croquet with the duke and duchess.

On my tenth day of confinement, a family of four took up residence in the room next to me — the hotel had only four rooms, divided by wallpapered membranes. I heard children sassing their parents and complaining they were bored. Denton had two sons in college and one married daughter. I wondered if I could influence them to move back home.

> *Email. Wednesday, July 3*
> Dent,
> Seems paradoxical to celebrate Independence Day while a prisoner in Idaho's inland Alcatraz. Elmer informs me that nothing much happens on July fourth. He says the big event is July fifth. Does that mean the Declaration of Independence took longer to arrive in Idaho?

No matter how miserable I was, I had to stick it out and make Denton pay for every day's lodging and meals. But the high mountains in every direction made me feel I was vacationing in a hole. I was like a boxer penned up in training camp and never allowed to fight. So I started scrutinizing everything and everyone. I forced myself to notice something different every day in order to still be able to plead sanity. At dinner, I practiced my method on the waiter. His name was Thomas. He told me not to order the halibut — didn't stay well frozen during shipping. Thomas stood beside people, hands folded, waiting for them to order if they took until next year.

I was drinking coffee outside the hotel the next morning. Elmer stepped out. "By gum, it's gonna' be a nice day."

"Yep," I said, but he didn't seem to catch my sarcasm. Since I was compiling information to remind myself I was alive, I asked, "How long you owned the hotel, Elmer?"

"Don't own it, just work here. Gives me something to do in retirement."

"Thought of moving away, now you're retired?"

"Why move? We've got telephones now and satellite television."

He stared off to the hills. If he was just going to stand there, I'd ask why Thomas stuck it out, too.

"Thomas? He's only been here four years. Attended Boise State a while. After he broke up with his fiancée he worked in McMahan a few months but it was too large for him. Been here ever since."

"Thomas doesn't seem the talkative kind. Did you do a background check when he applied for the job?"

"Nope."

"So he just told you about his fiancée?"

"Nope."

"How'd you know?"

"Whole town knows, but he didn't tell us."

"Elmer," I said, so he'd look at me, "if he didn't tell you, yet everybody knows —"

"We learned it the first July fifth he worked here. Guess he'd broken up with his fiancée July fifth the year before. She found out he was here, drove up, came in, ordered a beer and threw it in his face. She's done that three years now. Expect she'll do it again."

"So that's the July fifth event."

"By gum, you're right. Everybody in town came last year. Expect they'll be here this year, too. Don't know what they'll do if the little lady doesn't return."

"I'm surprised he'd take it."

"Thomas is a surprising person. Does a lot for our little town, especially on Christmas Eve and Easter morning."

The next day, having read through the magazine box back to the November 1965, issue of *Mechanix Illustrated*, I looked at the books Denton foisted on me. I might as well do the New Testament. I knew a lot of it already, since I'd watched television programs about the Bible, and I knew you could use the Bible to justify anything. I skimmed the first pages to get into the solid red font. Blessed this and blessed that. You have heard it said. Ah yes, "An eye for an eye and a tooth for a tooth." Just what I'll tell Denton. Then it angled off in a different direction. "But I say to you, Do not resist an evildoer. But if anyone strikes you on the right cheek, turn the other also." That ended my reading with a thump.

If I were to return to Portland to contend with Denton, I'd better build my physical strength. I started hiking on the trail near Cemetery Hill. A three-inch lizard zipped in front of me and a flecked hawk circled. Not ten minutes on the twisting trail, I heard barking and cussing ahead and a fellow came, chasing his dogs. I stepped aside. He ran by cussing and screaming, "Clancy! Kelly! Get back here!"

I said, "So this is hiking at a classy mountain resort," and followed the trail another fifty yards to come face-to-face with a cougar. It froze and so did I, except for my shaking legs. It was shiny, a light tan, and its face looked human — and mean. Calculated at emotional time we stared at one another for three-and-a-half hours. Clock time was less than two seconds and it was gone. It's hard to run while constantly looking back. I tried to calm myself by quipping, "Very interesting wildlife display," but it didn't work. My knees kept buckling. For the next couple hours I was unhinged. Such a small thing, I kept telling myself. Then I'd suddenly shake helplessly, feeling I should defend myself.

> *Email. Friday, July 5, 3 p.m.*
> Denton,
> *Following instructions, I've been reading. Also hiking — for my fallen belly problem. Encountered dangerous forest predator and barely escaped with my life.*

At dusk, the villagers started arriving at the restaurant. Nothing festive as one would expect so close to Independence Day. They came as though to view a case in court — or watch an execution. A lady said quietly to her husband, "I hope she doesn't show up."

Thomas served tables. At about 8:30, the sound of an approaching car quieted the place. Everyone faced the door when a cute, young woman walked in. She had black hair, a red tank top, and a small tattoo on her left shoulder. Thomas walked to her table as to any other.

"Hello, Pep."

"Hello Tom," she said, placing $2 on the table. "A Budweiser."

Thomas said nothing. He turned, and nineteen people watched him go to the bar and draw a beer. But I looked at her. Her eyes seemed as brown and helpless as the elk that smashed my car, but the rest of her face made me think of the cougar, and I'd rather brave the cougar. Thomas turned from the bar with the beer. I thought of Gary Cooper in *High Noon*. I wished Thomas would refuse to serve her, argue with her. I'd throw it at her!

She took the beer and stood up. "Happy July fifth, Tom," tossed it in his face, and left immediately. Thomas wiped his face with his apron as he walked to the bar, then back with a towel. On his hands and knees he cleaned the floor around the empty table and around the feet of the people where beer ran downhill.

Within fifteen minutes, everyone had quietly departed and I went up to my room. I sat dazed on the edge of the bed. I was staring at the three books on the nightstand, when the diesel generator rumbled to a stop. In bed, I watched the light of the moon advance slowly from one side of the room to the other. When I slept, it wasn't soundly. Thomas was standing with beer dripping down his cheeks or was on the floor with a towel, swabbing customers' feet, and always a cougar stared him in the face, but he didn't flinch. In my fully awake moments, I realized that nothing had bothered me like this. Why didn't he fight? Was he planning to get her back?

I was waiting when Thomas came to work the next afternoon. I stood when he walked in. "Thomas," I mumbled, "I'm sorry about last night."

"It's okay."

"I mean I'm really sorry."

Thomas patted me on the forearm. "It's really okay," he said, and he smiled slightly.

"Even though you knew what she was going to do?"

"Yes, but it's okay. Know what I mean?"

"No. I don't."

"I was engaged to Pep and I broke our engagement, but only after I first tried to nudge her to cancel the wedding plans. She said I owed her the truth and why didn't I just throw a beer in her face?"

"That's pretty rough, in front of everybody," I said. "How about not showing up? Or somehow fighting back?"

"Pep fights back. What good does it do her or anyone?"

I didn't answer.

"And it could be a lot worse," he said.

"Hard to imagine worse."

"She doesn't hurt me. Really hurt me."

He paused. He could tell I wasn't following him. He took a different tack. "I suppose it sounds simplistic, but I've realized you need a good reason to live, something important to measure your life by, compare yourself to."

"Yeah, but what can you compare to beer in the eyes?"

"To what Jesus suffered."

"It doesn't seem ... ah ... quite the same."

"It's hardly the same at all, but it's enough the same. I haven't always lived by it, but I do now. I appreciate your concern. By the lines in your forehead, you don't understand."

No, I didn't, exactly, but kind of. I told him I'd think about it, and I did, spending another night watching the moon's path across my room. I heard the reruns of Denton's lecture. Now the cougar faced me, and complained about how I treated people. I asked what would give me a good enough reason to do anything differently.

The next day was Sunday. I finally got up and I flipped the light switch but nothing happened. I had just grabbed the flashlight when I heard a diesel's slow start and the light flickered on. I stood in the middle of the little room and looked at my few clothes and the three books — New Testament on top. No, I didn't thoroughly understand Thomas, but I understood enough about what he possessed and I didn't. I could stay three more days here, but I'd be wasting Denton's money. If I drove all day I could be home tonight and start the week at work. I wouldn't tell Denton I'd read his books, but that I'd started and I'd finish.

While I'd been in Darrien, some kind state worker had graded the thirty miles of gravel down to McMahan. In order to stay awake I decided to count the waterfalls from Idaho's mountains to Portland; but when I drove by the place where the elk hit me, I imagined what my expression must have been and I chuckled. Then I passed where the flood had trapped me on the roof of the car. I kept laughing for miles, completely losing the ability to count.

Discussion Questions

1. What immediate responses do you have to the story?

2. Do you identify with a character in the story? If yes, how and why do you identify with the person? If no, why don't you identify with anyone in the story?

3. Would you like to have a conversation with a character in the story? What would you say, ask, or suggest to the person? Why?

4. How does the story bring the biblical text into a clearer focus for you?

5. How would you improve or modify the story? Why?

6. Since the story takes place near Independence Day, how do you suppose Keith understood independence/freedom at the beginning of the story, at the end of the story, three months after the story?

7. Have you given a person a second chance? Have you received a second chance? What happened in each case?

8. How have you been affected by another's difficult obedience to Christ?

9. What further depths of meaning, symbols, connections with, or applications of the biblical faith do you find in this story?

10. Since Jesus Christ has risen from the dead and is alive among us through the Holy Spirit, what of this story would you like Christ to activate in your life?

Chapter 10

By What Authority?

Mark 1:21-28

"Hillel or Shammai. Hillel or Shammai." It seemed to the two hired men toiling in the boat's stern that was all they heard from their bosses anymore. One hired man hauled in the net and whispered to the other, "I liked it better when they just argued about where to fish." He looked quickly over his shoulder at his two bosses quarreling in boat's bow. "I'm ready to join the Roman legions to get away from this."

"Hillel or Shammai." Those names had split the air over Galilee's lake for two weeks. The other hired man grabbed a trash fish by the tail, swung it, mashed its head against the boat, and tossed it in the water. "If I'd known their pilgrimage to Passover would bring this, I'd have drowned them first."

All the lake's fishermen knew that Johanan and Kostai argued as much as fished. How was it possible for brothers to be inseparable, but always disagreeing? To compound their problems these fishing partners, for the first time in their lives, journeyed to Jerusalem for Passover. They spent a week there having their ideas of religion confirmed by the disciples of their favorite teachers. In person they listened to teaching they'd heard about in fragments for years.

Kostai, predictably by his gentler nature, was inspired by Hillel's disciples. No one was astonished to discover that Johanan, matching his stern disposition, was as smitten by Shammai's approach to the faith as Kostai was to Hillel's. Their three-day journey back to Galilee wasn't pleasant for anyone in the caravan. Kostai argued for Hillel's more merciful interpretation of the law and Johanan claimed Shammai's more rigid method.

As Kostai struggled now around the boatload of fish toward the hired men in the stern, Johanan took his chance to talk to Kostai's back. "Hillel the Babylonian was taught by Shemaiah. Hillel is the prince of interpreters — reasonable, consistent, second only to Moses as the true authority in knowing God."

Johanan, a step away from the hired men, flung his head around so fast that he almost fell onto the nets. "Shammai," he shouted. "Shammai was taught by Menahem. Hillel bends the law into loops. Shammai explains the genuine intention of the holy writings." The hired men kept their heads down toward their work. They had their own opinion of Hillel and Shammai but it wasn't based on formal study.

Two days before, Peter and Andrew were casting their hand nets west of Capernaum's docks. They heard the brothers' quarrel. The names "Hillel" and "Shammai" echoed around the lake. Peter yelled over to Andrew, "Who says Galileans don't care about the finer points of Moses' law?"

On the first sabbath after Kostai and Johanan returned from Jerusalem, they were the first worshipers to show up at the synagogue for sabbath worship. After the Torah's reading, the two spoke first. They spoke most. They spoke last. Everyone in town knew just where each stood on matters of purity, blessings, acceptable reasons for divorce, tithes, and postures for reciting prayers.

On the next sabbath, so many people were gossiping about the brothers that they hardly noticed another teacher arrive in town. Most people didn't see Jesus enter the synagogue with Peter and Andrew and two of the town's other fishermen who, until the day before, had worked the lake just as hard as Johanan and Kostai.

Today the worshipers gathered as much to watch the brothers make fools of themselves as to hear the holy scriptures. Immediately after the Torah reading, Johanan was getting up to speak when Kostai, getting up also, bumped him and Johanan tumbled sideways, nearly falling onto a man's lap. Johanan was so amazed that he tried to slap Kostai while getting up again.

Before either could fully rise and face their fellow worshipers, the traveling rabbi stood. He immediately received more courteous attention than the two brothers. The longer Jesus explained the scripture, the less anyone wanted to hear Kostai or Johanan, even if they previously agreed with one of them. People were saying, "Yes, uh huh," as Jesus spoke. Others nodded their heads. Some stroked their beard or cradled their chin in their hand. Jesus didn't quote other teachers. He talked about the good news of God's coming kingdom and the need to repent — a regular John the Baptist. Johanan looked at Kostai. Both were confused. Jesus didn't argue with anyone's viewpoint.

After Jesus' teaching, Johanan stood and braced himself against a pillar, "The teacher Shammai," he mumbled, "would say that, ah —"

Then, the unclean spirit burst through a man's voice, "What have you to do with us, Jesus of Nazareth? Have you come to destroy us? I know who you are, the holy one of God." Jesus wouldn't debate with him, either. Jesus rebuked him, saying, "Be silent, and come out of him!" And the unclean spirit, convulsing him and crying with a loud voice, came out of him.

Kostai slowly rose and looked around at the people who were still starring at Jesus. "Well, Hillel, said —"

He stopped with a surprised look. Johanan sitting beside him was tugging at his sleeve. He was pulling his brother to sit him down. Johanan said loudly enough for everyone to hear, "Sit down and shut up. This guy knows what he's doing and what he's talking about. He really *is* an authority."

Kostai, without another word sat. For weeks to come, the folk around Capernaum talked as much of Johanan and Kostai's being silenced as about Jesus' casting out the demon. For one reason or the other, Jesus' fame began to spread throughout the surrounding region of Galilee. Also, fishing on the lake was a lot quieter.

Discussion Questions

1. What immediate responses do you have to the story?

2. Do you identify with a character in the story? If yes, how and why do you identify with the person? If no, why don't you identify with anyone in the story?

3. Would you like to have a conversation with a character in the story? What would you say, ask, or suggest to the person? Why?

4. How does the story bring the biblical text into a clearer focus for you?

5. How would you improve or modify the story? Why?

6. Have you dealt with rigid believers who exclude as legitimate any other religious viewpoint? What was the experience like? Have you done so yourself?

7. Have you had an experience in which you realized that Jesus' personal authority extends beyond sectarian narrowness?

8. How would you describe and explain the authority that people perceive in Jesus?

9. What further depths of meaning, symbols, connections with, or applications of the biblical faith do you find in the story?

10. Since Jesus Christ has risen from the dead and is alive among us through his Holy Spirit, what of this story would you like Christ to activate in your life?

Chapter 11

Jerusalem From The West

Mark 1:40-44; Psalm 125:2; Isaiah 53:7-8

Note for reading aloud: Before the story, help the listeners memorize Psalm 125:2. When encountering Psalm 125:2 in the story, the reader signals to the listeners to repeat the verse together: "As the mountains surround Jerusalem, so the Lord surrounds his people, from this time on and forevermore."

* * *

Over the next rise, he thought. But it wasn't over the next rise. The next one, he thought, as his wobbly old legs carried him slowly higher; but no, Jerusalem didn't appear. Yose had never approached Jerusalem from the west. Over every little mount he expected to see the city that had been his favorite. He had lived in Syrian Antioch for the last thirty years and it had been 32 years since he last saw Jerusalem. It had also been 32 years since he served there as priest. Although he might be recognized, he assumed he was safe. What would it be like, if he were to enter the place he once thought was the center of the world — Jerusalem's temple?

Yose's earliest memory was of Jerusalem's temple. On the eastern crest of the Mount of Olives his father had stopped the caravan, hefted Yose onto his shoulders, and ascended the last few paces to the summit to gaze upon Jerusalem and its holy temple. " 'As the mountains surround Jerusalem, so the Lord surrounds his people, from this time on and forevermore.' Repeat that, Yose."

Yose stumbled with the words. His father helped him repeat: " 'As the mountains surround Jerusalem, so the Lord surrounds his people, from this time on and forevermore.' Always remember this moment. You were born to serve in this temple." His father pointed across the Kidron ravine to the structure 100 times larger than any Yose had ever seen.

"When you crest the last hill to Jerusalem repeat the psalm, 'As the mountains surround Jerusalem, so the Lord surrounds his people, from this time on and forevermore.'"

Yose had remained in Jerusalem for the week his father served in the temple. All he remembered of that first visit was the temple, he was born to serve the Lord there, and the psalm, "As the mountains surround Jerusalem, so the Lord surrounds his people, from this time on and forevermore."

A few years later, he viewed for the first time a sheep sacrificed in the temple. The knife was so sharp that, when the artery on its neck was cut, the animal hardly flinched. From only a few paces away Yose watched the animal stumble to its knees, then fall upon its side, eyes wide, legs quivering.

When he was twenty, he was examined by the Sanhedrin in the temple's Chamber of Hewn Stone and was found physically fit for ordination. He remembered the awesome ceremonies of bathing and receiving his priestly clothing and then the week's series of sacrifices. He vividly recalled the first sacrifice he administered, the first time he stood beside the Levites who cut the sheep's neck and the first time he sprinkled blood upon the giant altar's horns — blood landing upon his white, priestly garments. Yose could never imagine anything as wonderful as being a priest in his Lord's temple.

Yose worked for his cousin, constructing and repairing everything from tools to buildings. He married and his first child was a son. Yose's joy was the same with his son as his father's with him. He was most happy when preparing his son for the service that only males of certain families were born for: ministering as the Lord's priest in the temple, the holiest spot on earth. He warned his son as his father warned him, "Always be careful around yoked animals. It's not just that oxen can cripple you so you can't work. If you're crippled you become blemished and can't serve in the temple."

Yose now climbed toward Jerusalem from the west. How differently he considered the temple today than on that evening 32 years before. That evening he returned home from a day of patching roofs to find a man awaiting him.

"You're Yose?"

"Yes."

"I was told in the last village you're a priest."

"Yes," Yose said, setting down his bag of tools by the door of his house.

"I need a priest to declare me clean of leprosy."

"Good you found me tonight. It's half a day's walk to another priest. You are?"

"My name's Nittai."

Yose didn't mind working for his cousin, but he preferred priestly duties. How wonderful if he were high priest in Jerusalem serving at the Lord's altar whenever he wanted. Yet, Yose was an ordinary priest serving one week twice a year with his division of priests and three times a year with all priests at the three pilgrim festivals.

He said cheerfully, "Let's go where I can see well." Yose called into the house that he was back and needed the lamp outside for a preliminary inspection of a leper. Yose's son and daughter brought the lighted lamp and carefully kept their father between them and the leper.

"Take off your sash."

"Gladly."

Yose looked at the man's arms and torso, neck and head.

"As far as I can tell, Nittai, you look fine. Your skin seems normal. But we must wait until full sunlight. Where do you live?"

"I've traveled two days from lower Galilee."

"Do you have kin near?"

"No."

"See those olive trees? The children will get you some straw so you can sleep under them."

The next day Yose pronounced him clean, and Nittai bounded with joy. Yose asked, "How long have you been stricken?"

"Half a year. My whole torso was splotched."

Yose marveled at the man's recovery and asked how it occurred.

"A holy man named Jesus visited our village and I went right to him, kneeled and begged him saying, 'If you choose, you can make me clean.' 'I do choose,' he said in a very compassionate way. 'Be made clean.' And he touched me."

"Touched you?"

"Yes," Nittai said, laughing. "I've told everybody, but they don't believe me."

"Touched you while you were unclean?"

"Truly. He touched me and I was immediately cleansed." Nittai laughed so hard he hiccupped. "I can't explain what it will be like to hold my wife and children again, to enter my house, to eat with the family. It's God's deed. I don't care what anybody thinks. Jesus did it with a touch."

Yose didn't doubt Nittai, but if someone healed him by touch, the touching rendered the healer himself unclean. Yose didn't think further about it because he was almost as happy as Nittai. From his earliest days he watched his father inspect people's skin, and often the person wasn't wholly well. The same happened with Yose. He inspected people, yet too often in order to report the sad news that they must remain excluded from the community.

Yose sent Nittai on to the Jerusalem temple, instructing him to wait at the temple's Nicanor Gate for a priest to inspect him again and instruct him on the prescribed ritual. Nothing was out of the ordinary in his certifying Nittai clean and sending him to Jerusalem for the temple rituals, except, perhaps, that Nittai repeated Jesus' instructions, "Go, show yourself to the priest, and offer for your cleansing what Moses commanded, as a witness to them."

Nine weeks later Yose had joined 300 priests, 400 Levites, and a lay delegation of 100 men walking to the temple for their week's service. It was the end of an excessively hot summer. The five-day walk was grueling. Many of the elder priests collapsed. Small groups of men were strung out along the road from Jericho to Jerusalem with half a day's walk separating the first from the last. They climbed the hill to Jerusalem in stages, stopping often. Dust clung to their damp clothes. No matter how they rationed it, their water skins were empty too soon. Yose was young and strong, yet he had to command his legs to take each step. Finally, cresting the Mount of Olives, he gasped, "As the mountains surround Jerusalem, so the Lord surrounds his people, from this time on and forevermore."

In Jerusalem heat reflected off buildings. People sat in the streets, panting in the shade. Yose and his group anticipated the temple pools as much for the physical refreshment as for the ritual cleansing. But as they approached the temple steps, a guard was asking every priest if he knew Yose.

"I'm Yose," he said, confused and fearful.

"Come with me."

Yose looked blankly at his friends as he gestured good-bye to them. He asked, "Where're we going?"

"To the high priest."

"I'm exhausted," Yose said. "I don't know if I can walk much farther."

"Over there," the guard pointed. "Not even half a sabbath day's walk."

While he waited in the high priest's courtyard, he asked a slave for a drink. He received no response and no drink. When he'd stumbled toward the temple steps, he didn't believe he could become hotter or thirstier, but now he was. He tried to think about the holy service awaiting him in the temple.

Two men in fine clothing led him inside to Caiaphas, who was reclining upon pillows. Three slaves slowly flapped garments to cool him. They looked like bakers shooing flies from bread dough. Caiaphas gazed upon Yose for a long time before speaking. Caiaphas was panting slightly from the heat, and his bulbous eyebrows held drops of sweat. He spoke slowly. "You are Yose?"

"Yes, my lord."

"Did you declare the cleansing of a leper named Nittai?"

Yose's very thinking swayed in the heat, but he recalled the man clearly. "Yes, my lord."

The men who brought Yose to Caiaphas stood beside the high priest, and all three glowered at Yose in silence. A puddle formed from Yose's sweat. Caiaphas summoned a slave into the room with a goblet of water. He ordered the slave to stand beside Yose. Yose looked into the clean water. His mind tottered. He seemed to be dreaming.

"As you recall, was anything irregular about the leper's cleansing?"

Yose did his best to remember the details: "He said he was healed instantly. The person who did it, named Jesus, touched him, and Nittai was very grateful."

Caiaphas rubbed his hands together as though removing chaff from wheat. "Anything strange about Nittai's skin?"

"No. I examined him carefully in full sunlight."

Caiaphas glanced to the man on his right, who took his cue. "Yose, could you have been incorrect?"

"No, my lord."

"Could you have been mistaken in any way about the leper Nittai's health?"

"No, my lord."

"You are perfect in all your observations?"

"My lord, since a lad I've observed the examination of lepers. I saw my father accept or reject lepers as cleansed. I judged —"

"You were wrong about Nittai," Caiaphas cut him off.

"Wrong? If he was leprous when he arrived in Jerusalem, my lord, I swear by the stones in the Lord's temple that —"

"Enough," said the third man, who stepped nearer, frowning. "You must confess your error. I've written a document to that effect and you must sign it."

The room was heavy with heat. Yose could even feel his hair, hot on his head; but through his confusion and discomfort he was able to say, "I testify to you he was clean." Then he fainted.

He awoke lying on a cool floor and shackled to a wall. He could hear sounds above and he saw a dim light under a door. That evening he again stood before Caiaphas. This time Caiaphas was flanked by seven others.

"We are granting you, Yose, a chance to retract your testimony."

"On what, my lord?"

"You pronounced as clean a leper who claimed that the renegade, Jesus, healed him."

"My lord, the man was clean of leprosy, every portion of his skin. But I forgot one thing. Jesus told Nittai to see a priest and to offer what Moses commanded, as a witness to them."

The men looked at one another. A heavily bearded man spoke. "There've been some problems at the temple archive, Yose. We've not been able to find record of your son's being registered for the priesthood. How old is he?"

"Twelve."

"Will you acknowledge your mistake? If so, we'll order the records searched again."

Yose had disembarked at the port of Caesarea. He had climbed toward Jerusalem for four days. His steps were slow but he strained urgently to gain the last summit. This was surely it, yes! He stared down upon Jerusalem from the west. From many years before the words issued from him. "As the mountains surround Jerusalem, so the Lord surrounds his people, from this time on and forevermore." The temple lay before him, with porticoes on a raised platform, the culmination of the elder Herod's rebuilding project. Yose had seen Herod's contribution to opulence at Syrian Antioch. He wasn't impressed in Antioch, and now he was uneasy, seeing the temple the elder Herod had built. He wondered how it would impress him if he entered.

Yose hadn't understood at the time why he was treated so badly by Caiaphas; yet, even realizing that his male descendants would be excluded from serving as priests and disqualified from a priest's income, he didn't lie. His decision barred him from entering the Priests' Court. He had wandered home to try to explain to his family what happened and to set to work building furniture, repairing walls, carving yokes; but sadness slowed his every movement. Especially he was melancholy when his priestly division was serving in the temple.

He didn't return to Jerusalem, nor did his family, but two years later they listened intently to the preachers who began visiting their village to announce that Jesus of Nazareth was killed in Jerusalem at the behest of the chief priests. Yose believed Caiaphas capable of such. However, the preachers announced that Jesus was raised to new life as he promised and that Jesus' risen body was the new temple. Yose was wary until one preacher explained that the scripture prophesied about Jesus, "He was oppressed, and he was afflicted, yet he did not open his mouth; like a lamb that is led to the slaughter, and like a sheep that before its shearers is silent, so he did not open his mouth. By a perversion of justice he was taken away. Who could have imagined his future? For he was cut off from the land of the living, stricken for the transgression of my people."

Yose knew how sheep were slaughtered in the temple, and he experienced that the innocent sometimes suffered and that justice was perverted. Now the message about Jesus made sense. Within a few months he parted from his cousin and, along with his wife, son, and daughter he followed the Christian missionaries to Syrian Antioch. There he learned how the new Christian faith fulfilled the Hebrew scriptures. He trained as a teacher and loyally served the Christians in the Roman province of Cilicia and Syria. Now, as an old man, his wife dead, his son and daughter each married and traveling as Christian missionaries, the Christian community in Syrian Antioch sent Yose back to Jerusalem as a former priest who could teach and encourage the few Jewish Christians left there.

Yose knew the directions to Jerusalem's Christian gatherings, yet he stopped to gaze upon his once beloved temple precincts — the enormous stones, the decorated walls — and he knew that beyond was the awesome holy place in front of which he had watched sheep slaughtered and had himself splashed blood on the altar. From half a lifetime ago, he could visualize the priests busy at the altar, see the dead sheep hanging on hooks, hear the Levites singing. He didn't plan to enter, but the memories of his father, the yearnings for his familiar duty, and his wondering about what this building now meant for his Christian faith led him on. He ascended the massively wide steps, and, mingling with the crowds, entered the temple at the time of the evening sacrifice.

People around him spoke foreign languages. Worshipers exchanged coins at the money changers' tables. Beneath gigantic colonnades rabbis taught groups of students. Yose smelled fresh blood and burning flesh. Encircled by humanity, he shouldered ever closer through the Gentiles' court, then up into the women's court. Slowly the final steps up to Israel's court. Closer he nudged, advancing toward the priests' court. Men bumped him. He hardly felt them. Beyond a couple more groups of men the holy place itself rose before him. He stepped closer anytime someone near him moved. The horns of the massive altar loomed above the crowd. Another step and he saw the top of the altar's ramp. He restrained his hurrying through the crowd with stuttering steps, until finally he faced squarely the priests' court as they brought the sheep for sacrifice.

He seemed in a dream of memory as he watched the ritual he hadn't witnessed for three decades. A Levite cut the sheep's throat. Yose stood rigidly still. A priest caught its blood and cast it upon the altar. Yose's breathing was shallow. The sheep's blood spilled on the priest as he tossed it high upon the altar, and the remainder trickled into the gutter. His stomach turned. He mumbled, "Like my Lord Jesus."

Yose didn't belong here. He had thoughtlessly entered the temple, disregarding that he might be recognized and ejected. He could bear the punishment if his fellow Jews identified him, but he didn't want to be seen here by his fellow Christians. He scurried out of the temple, breathing heavily. He rushed through Jerusalem's streets, as though repelled by an edifice and a holiness enterprise that was more than worn out and ineffective. It was repulsive.

He hastened to his Christian brothers and sisters. He had memorized ten of their names. They were Jesus' new temple, and their risen Lord was surely surrounding his new people here in Jerusalem. Yose's intent, now more pressing than anything he ever felt, was to find them so he could tell them that, although he hadn't known them previously, they now meant more to him than any building he had ever seen.

Discussion Questions

1. What immediate responses do you have to the story?

2. Do you identify with a character in the story? If yes, how and why do you identify with the person? If no, why don't you identify with anyone in the story?

3. Would you like to have a conversation with a character in the story? What would you say, ask, or suggest to the person? Why?

4. How does the story bring the biblical text into a clearer focus for you?

5. How would you improve or modify the story? Why?

6. Does church architecture help your faith? Do you respond positively to large, beautiful church buildings? Why or why not?

7. How has it been necessary for you to "leave" part of your faith as Yose did? How did your "leaving" prove to be positive? How was it negative?

8. Yose journeyed 300 miles north of Jerusalem to live in Antioch on the Orontes for thirty years before returning to Jerusalem. Has your faith been at all like a journey that took you away from your home and then brought you home again, but as a different person?

9. What further depths of meaning, symbols, connections with, or applications of the biblical faith do you find in the story?

10. Since Jesus Christ has risen from the dead and is alive among us through his Holy Spirit, what of this story would you like Christ to activate in your life?

Emphasis or special occasion: Prayer

Chapter 12

Althea Genler's Subtle Memorial Blessing

Mark 4:10-12; Jude 24-25

We are gathered today to remember and to celebrate the life of Althea Sturm Genler. She was extraordinary by any standard. She was my dear friend and often my advisor. After I also moved to Oregon, I was privileged to know Max for three years and Althea for seven. They sort of adopted me as the child they never bore.

Althea, first with Max and me, and after his death, just with me, complained how pedantic, plodding, and predictable were the few sermons she heard in her youth. As we discussed the biblical message, she said, "Why don't preachers take the Bible as their form instead of just as content? The Bible is mostly stories, and interesting stories at that. It's filled with poetry, even an immortal drama in Job — not to mention the drama of the book of Revelation. Why so brutally literal all the time, constantly explaining everything, moralizing, every sermon sounding the same no matter what part of the Bible its text? Jesus was more flexible, doing his best teaching with parables. God doesn't merely give commandments. Sometimes God gives provocative suggestions." You can probably hear Althea say that. English teacher through and through.

Granting Althea's wishes, you've heard this morning two Bible texts: one about the obscurity of Jesus' teaching and the other a blessing from Jude. She insisted upon Jesus' saying that his parables were hard to understand. She said, "It's my funeral and they're my friends. Let them figure it out. If they can't figure it out, bless them anyway." I'm sure you hear her voice behind those words, too.

In Althea's memory, I share with you the funeral meditation she and I planned together over the last eight months. Her dictating, my writing. Here follows "Althea Genler's Subtle Memorial Blessing," as she titled it, crafted first over coffee and Oreos in her breakfast nook and finally beside her hospital bed.

Althea Sturm stood beside her shiny Honda Accord, gray, 4,700 miles on the odometer. It had been packed for an hour. Althea was always early, the result of her German genes, she said. She leaned against the car, looking at her watch, waiting. From excitement she hadn't slept well for three nights.

Montana's late summer morning was already warm. The violent thunderstorms, the gully-washers of the week before, only made it hotter with increased humidity. What an irrational time to begin public school instruction — the same mystery she'd pondered for each of the forty previous Montana autumns.

Althea listened for fall's first bell to ring at Custer County District High School. She always had an apartment near the school. So, from her home she always heard the cars of the early students. She informed Marla Huffman that on the first day of school all students with automobiles drove to school. If their family had two automobiles, on the first day of school the student would somehow drive both. Last week, Marla Huffman moved into the classroom that Althea taught in for 22 years, and this morning Marla, too, was waiting, only inside Custer County District High School instead of outside.

Althea remembered last June's final bell of the spring. "Doom's high, trembling gong," she named it. Now, across the late summer morning, the bell finally announced the first day of school. Althea sighed, stepped into the car, looked back at her apartment, and drove two blocks to the high school. The marquee in front of the three-story brick building announced the first football game for the Custer County Cowboys — last year's state champs. She drove slowly, then stopped. Marla was at the window of Althea's old classroom. They waved. Althea mouthed, "Good-bye," and she was off on her great adventure.

She drove north on Highway 59, crossing the Yellowstone River's shallow, late summer flow. At the top of Airport Hill she glanced in her rearview mirror for her last sight of Miles City. It looked like an oasis against the brown hills that held it in the valley.

She was on the rolling plains, able upon a rise to see for twenty or thirty miles. She always felt expansive when she drove out of the Yellowstone Valley and onto the plains. When she first moved to Miles City, the spreading plains seemed barren and oppressive. Now, her being able to see for miles was freeing, but she didn't feel free.

"Am I really done?" Her voice in the car sounded fuller than speaking outside, not quite like singing in the shower, but enough change to sound as if she were speaking to someone, though she wasn't.

"Am I retired? I've the pension checks to prove that. But have I completed my task, learned all I should learn, taught all I should teach? I think not, but I am leaving, nonetheless."

Nearly two-thirds of her life ago she arrived in Miles City, Althea Sturm, graduate teacher. Across the decades she learned that the area she was driving in produced the richest grazing grass in the world — during wet cycles. During a dry cycle, the soil could blow five states away. Now she would explore more fully the eastern Montana plains that had surrounded her for four decades. She carried contingency plans for western North Dakota and potential forays into southern Saskatchewan. She even mused upon the different possibility, slim indeed, of driving to Oregon. Almost certainly she wouldn't continue to Oregon.

She planned to photograph the remains of old schoolhouses on the plains. Aided by the interlibrary loan, she spent her first summer of retirement eating on a TV-tray, because maps and books covered her dining table. Her intention was to leave upon the first day of school after retirement. And she did. She could hardly believe it. She often devised vacations: a week with a wagon train on the old Oregon Trail, rafting and camping down the Colorado River, backpacking in the Rockies. Although she ordered the brochures and made phone calls, her vacations were usually driving to Chicago to see family, taking summer courses at Eastern Montana or

Montana State, or just reading. A few times on her vacations she attempted to write a novel, but never finished.

Althea didn't regret not leaping out on great treks. Because the truth was, and you know it well, she loved two things above all: teaching and reading — whether it be the classics or science fiction, poetry or Gothic romances. Marla Huffman said that if the library issued frequent flyer miles for checking out books, Althea could have circled the globe nineteen dozen times.

Althea saw a few scattered wheat fields laid out in strips of fallow and planted, so straight north and south you could set Polaris by them. "All right. Milepost 46." She became alert. She wasn't going to forsake the main road to view new buildings, although a few elementary schools functioned out here, tucked away in the land's gentle folds. She planned to photograph the relics, the ruins. In some places she expected only a foundation's rock outline.

Four antelope to the left, and empty as far as she looked in every direction. People once lived here by the hundreds, after the railroads pressured Congress to pass the ill-fated Enlarged Homestead Act of 1909. Althea wasn't concerned about most that occurred upon these plains: that General Nelson A. Miles chased Indians at fifty below zero in the winter of 1876 to '77 to punish Custer's killers, or that the last buffalo of the great northern herd had been shot in 1886 near Jordan. She thought only of the homesteaders who came later, two families on every square mile: The communities, stores, and transfer companies that sprang up as hardworking, or desperate, or greedy, or stupid people came to take what they were told was free — or almost free; to stack sod for houses, or burrow caves into the ground, or tack tar paper onto shacks; to bust the sod with horses or mules or oxen; to work from morning until dark digging wells, building roads, even forming lodges; to cut and drag trees — always from far away; to string barbed wire, and make meals and bear children and wash clothes on Mondays; and to suffer all their labor blown away or eaten by grasshoppers in little over a decade.

Althea felt a painful kinship with those homesteaders. She taught their grandchildren and great-grandchildren. She viewed their photographs and inspected their tack and gramophones in the Range

Riders Museum. She came now to inspect their artifacts left behind at the focal point of combined labor and intentional civilization called "the schoolhouse."

She attended such a schoolhouse in her third grade, her childhood's only year not spent in Chicago. The school had two rooms and two teachers, not exactly on the plains, but nestled into a stubbly Nebraska woodland. The building, half a mile from the farm her parents failed at managing, was also used for worship — on Saturdays by Seventh Day Adventists and on Sundays by Baptists. Althea's parents sent her to one, then to the other, for a few weeks at a time. How strange to spend a week in the building learning longhand and multiplication, studying geography and history, and then to enter and encounter a few huddled Bible classes, followed by a preacher who always stood behind the desk to yell his sermon.

She much preferred school to church and told her parents so. Because they didn't attend and she could work a little for them on the weekends, they usually kept her out of church. When she was fourteen and living in Chicago again, she decided to keep herself out of church.

There, milepost 48. She slowed and turned east onto the red scoria gravel, the outcome of a burned underground coal seam now crushed and spread like a dirty pink line across the flats. It wasn't graded as well as most county roads, but it aimed straight: East/Northeast across a two-mile flat, then over a rise. It continued three miles on a flat only to ascend another rise that looked just like the last. Her directions weren't precise about this site. Not the way she wanted to start. But onward, her car seeming to steer itself on its straight course. She hummed a little, already imagining the dozens of sites to photograph and annotate for the album she would cherish for the rest of her life. She was contemplating possible colors for the album's cover as she crested the lowest of hills suddenly to meet a sharp turn to the right and on the left a reedy pond. Althea jammed on the brake and she spun the wheel to the right, skidding with an almost graceful, completely unstoppable slide, until the left front of her brand-new, shiny gray Honda Accord hit the mud at the pond's edge.

By training, Althea sat rigidly in her seat, although she wanted to go limp. Years of standing before uninterested or belligerent students held her erect when she'd rather slump. After a few deep breaths she shifted into reverse, yet the front wheels only spun and she felt the car sink instantly. She was surprised. She thought her front tires were on solid ground. She turned off the engine and opened her door. Water up to the floor. She slid across the seat and opened the passenger's door. She held onto the roof, then sprang out of the car onto what appeared nearly solid ground, but which wasn't.

Three steps out of the mess and her shoes were covered. "Gumbo," she said. Out here the clay was "gumbo," and people seldom spoke the word without a modifier, most often, "damned gumbo." She walked away from the car to examine the problem. The pond was 25 yards across and ringed with low hills. She compared it to a big brown saucer of mud with a car pasted on the edge, a car that wasn't coming out under its own power.

"Cell phone," she said, snapping her fingers. She stepped through the gumbo and leaped onto her knees on the front seat. Camera equipment lay in state upon the backseat, but in her tired muddle she'd forgotten the cell phone.

She held her muddy feet out the door and took off her shoes, banged them against the outside and closed the door to wait. Someone will come soon. She saw tire tracks from after the rain.

Doing nothing wasn't natural for Althea. She could be reading, but she didn't want to put on her shoes and wade to the trunk for a book. And she was tired. What could she do? She considered taking a photograph out the window as the first snapshot for her album, but decided she didn't want to explain it every time she showed her collection to someone.

She could pray. Of course. That's the thing to do. She didn't pray much, but she didn't have anything against God, even if she hadn't prayed for a few months or, honestly, for years. She cleared her throat as she folded her hands and bowed her head. "O Thou who wast ... O Thou who didst...." She swallowed. "O Thou who hast...." Nothing more, except that she could hear Max laughing at her. Forty-plus years away and she could still hear him laugh. Max

Genler was the closest she'd gotten to religion since she was fourteen. She met him junior year at the University of Chicago. He invited her to a Christian meeting, and she'd gone a few times — more because of interest in Max than in faith. A few times Max asked, "Althea, would you open us with prayer?" Or, "Will you close us with prayer, Althea?" She declined. But once the discussion was about prayer. She complained, "Why do you all take God so casually? You chat in your prayers. If you address God, you should be serious."

"I'm serious," Max said, and laughed.

"Well you don't sound like it, all chummy with the almighty. If you were introduced to the Queen of England you wouldn't say, 'Hi, Queen.'"

"You can be serious and intimate at the same time. Married people are."

"It's not the same, Max. If you're going to talk to God, it should sound a little more, well, intense, than a conversation over the back fence."

"Althea, if you pray in a fancy way, you'll only pray about fancy things. God *is* over the back fence. God is here in all of life, so why not take all of life to God in prayer — as you would to any friend?"

"You can't shrink God into a mere pal."

"But why not feel comfortable while speaking to God?"

"Comfortable? No, you should be absolutely alert so you can be severely honest."

"I think you should be comfortable, so comfortable that you can fall asleep praying."

"That's not comfort. That's sloth."

"Shouldn't you feel so safe with God that you can fall asleep with him, as you can fall asleep with a person you love?"

"No." Her voice became tight at the thought of sleeping with someone she loved. "Not with God. It's the greatest affront to demote God to little more than human."

"All right, then, show us how to pray." Max sat there grinning, arms crossed, and she didn't want him to get the better of her. She bowed her head with a snap, clasped her hands with the force of climbing a rope, and prayed, "O Thou who hast...."

Max started laughing. And you know that no one, not even Althea while attempting to prove a point, could withstand his laughter. She laughed, too.

Recently she'd thought a lot about Max, since she saw his name on the university's list of alumni contributors. She couldn't resist a search for his email address and writing a letter about herself, stating that she was now retiring, if still not shy.

Althea sat behind the wheel and concentrated her mind for prayer. "O Thou...."

Max had responded that very evening: an email telling of his two sons and one daughter, his wife, Leah's, death nine years before, his plan to move from southern California to Oregon in early spring — and an invitation to her to stretch her expedition to Oregon. After her years in the classroom, not much could surprise Althea; but, she waited four days to respond to "Maximum Genler," as his friends called him. She felt strange at her computer, touching the key to send this message to him. Maybe she loved Max in college. She didn't know. She grew up hearing her mother say, "Marry in haste, repent at leisure." When she was young she thought her mother was angry in saying it, but when she was older, her mother seemed only sad. Althea so feared marrying in haste that she never married.

She tried again, "O Thou Eternal Spirit...."

A man was knocking on the driver's window. "You okay?"

The sun was far in the west. She leaned away from the window and paused for a second, then rolled it down, "Yes, I fell asleep."

He was standing knee-deep in water.

"Want help out of the car?"

"I've gotten out once. I was waiting for someone to come by."

"I'll help you out. This is quite a loblolly. Come to the other side." He circled to the right of the car. Althea opened the door and handed him her shoes. He hefted her out of the car and onto dry ground in about two seconds. Max had lifted her once, and she'd liked that.

"I was so used to the road being straight," Althea said quickly, "and I came over this hill, and here's a pond."

"Uh huh. You get used to 'straight' and suddenly you hit the labyrinthine ways."

Althea, listening politely while looking at the condition of her car, jerked her head toward him. "Labyrinthine ways?"

"Like Francis Thompson's poem."

"Yes, but, but —"

"One of the poems in your class: 'The Hound of Heaven,' about not being able to flee God."

"You know me?"

"You're Miss Sturm. I recognized you from your picture in the *Star* when you retired."

"Oh," Althea said. She'd been lifted out of her car by a man who knew her but whom she didn't know.

"I'm Henry Anderson, Anderson with 'oh en.' Hank." They shook hands. "You had both my kids in school: Carl and Marie."

"Yes."

"On spring vacation, Carl memorized the poem by reciting it every night and three times on the Sunday before he went back to school. I guess we learned it with him."

"Carl was one of my favorite students."

Hank Anderson smiled until his teeth looked like the grill on a '55 Buick.

"But I thought Carl and Marie lived in town."

"With my brother, Sam. They stayed with him and my sister-in-law so they could live in Miles and attend Custer."

"So you didn't see your children much during the school year."

"Just on vacations and a few weekends; but we all agreed, my wife and I and the kids. They wanted to attend Custer, and especially your class."

Althea stepped back. She stood erect. She felt weak.

"Their cousins, Rosalyn and Derek, told them about you," Hank said. "They wanted to be in your class. The four cousins all liked to read and write. Carl became editor of the University of Montana's *Kaimin*. He's now staff writer for the *Great Falls Tribune*."

"He sent me a graduation announcement and I mailed him congratulations."

"He showed us your card."

For once Althea didn't have anything to say.

"I can hook on and get you out in a minute," Hank said, pointing to his flatbed truck. It sat idling with half a load of hay bales. She put on her shoes and Hank carried her back to the car, setting her down as gently as a nurse placing a newborn in an incubator. He drove behind, connected a chain, and the car was quickly out and undamaged.

"I very much appreciate your help Mr. Anderson. I didn't know if anyone lived on this road."

"We do. A couple miles farther. My family has lived here over ninety years. Would you come up for dinner?" He cocked his head toward his home with the question. "Alice would love to put on another plate."

"No, no," Althea said, "I've got a long ways to go yet, and it's getting late." Like a native she nodded to the sun instead of looking at her watch.

They shook hands.

"Oh," she said as she turned to leave, "is there an old schoolhouse down this road?"

"No."

"Ever been a schoolhouse down this road?"

"No."

"Well, thank you again."

"I couldn't have been happier to meet you."

Arriving back at Highway 59, she turned off the engine. One whole day gone and no schoolhouse. Nearly a ruinous accident. Failed completely on the first attempt. It was 6:40. Considering the energy needed to travel, maybe she should return to Miles City, sleep in her own bed, get her cell phone, maybe take a couple days for further inquiries about the schoolhouse she missed. She looked south toward home.

She started the car and accelerated faster than usual — going north. She set her cruise control at 73 and didn't look in her rearview mirror. At milepost 65, she passed the big rocks set up as corner posts for fences. She could stay in Jordan. Since no game was in season, the Garfield Hotel & Motel would have a room.

"Well Lord, I guess the teaching was a good thing, and it's nice to find that out, if only afterward. Let's see if retirement will be a good thing, too. And, Lord, what do you think about Oregon?"

Max and Althea are now with God and that's a comfort. Time is God's gift to help heal our grief. But I'm sure that for the rest of my life whenever I hear an older couple laughing, I'll still miss Max and Althea.

Althea directed that this service end with a blessing from Jude. I thought she'd want it from the King James Bible — good Elizabethan language. "No," she said, "the blessing is for my friends and relatives. Let them hear it in their language. Bless them, even if they haven't understood my story. That's how God treated me all my life."

Receive God's blessing from our friend, Althea Sturm Genler. "Now to him who is able to keep you from falling, and to make you stand without blemish in the presence of his glory with rejoicing, to the only God our Savior, through Jesus Christ our Lord, be glory, majesty, power, and authority, before all time and now and forever. Amen."

Discussion Questions

1. What immediate responses do you have to the story?

2. Do you identify with a character in the story? If yes, how and why do you identify with the person? If no, why don't you identify with anyone in the story?

3. Would you like to have a conversation with a character in the story? What would you say, ask, or suggest to the person? Why?

4. How does the story bring the biblical text into a clearer focus for you?

5. How would you improve or modify the story? Why?

6. Has a special friend helped you understand prayer?

7. Have you struggled between formal and informal language in prayer? What have you most recently experienced or learned of prayer?

8. Has God used some particularly twisted circumstances to lead you to deeper faith? If you've read Francis Thompson's poem, "The Hound of Heaven," what connections do you see between the poem and Althea's story?

9. What further depths of meaning, symbols, connections with, or applications of the biblical faith do you find in the story?

10. Since Jesus Christ has risen from the dead and is alive among us through his Holy Spirit, what of this story would you like Christ to activate in your life?

Chapter 13

Jesus' Questions

Mark 9:30-37

"You learned fast that you didn't want Jesus asking you questions," Peter said as he and his students walked through a market in Antioch. "As long as Jesus was speaking to others or just talking and not asking questions, we could smile and nod our heads like we really understood and agreed with him. We'd gotten good at it. When he started asking questions, you wanted to duck and not meet his eye."

As an apostle who'd been with Jesus and seen him after his resurrection, Peter was the center of every Christian group he visited. His Syrian students swarmed around him through the market's crowd. Peter wouldn't be in Antioch much longer, so he took every occasion to teach, continuing now to instruct them as he walked.

"Jesus would ask questions like, 'If a shepherd has 100 sheep, and one of them has gone astray, does he not leave the 99 on the mountains and go in search of the one that went astray?' You figured out soon that somehow what Jesus said, as ordinary as it was on the face of it, had a hook. Almost certainly he'd get around to you and God and your attitude toward others. He'd confuse us by asking ridiculous questions like, 'Is a lamp brought in to be put under a bushel basket?' We'd all stand there scratching our heads. Sometimes if you waited long enough, he'd answer his own question. So, we got used to ignoring such things.

"If we didn't understand what he was talking about, it was better not to bring it up. If he thought you hadn't understood what he was getting at, he'd sting you with his reply. He was tough that way. But we knew Jesus was bound for greatness and we were willing to put up with his quirks. He'd get straightened out as he realized what he could accomplish with his popularity. We were his closest associates and we'd advise him in embarrassing situations and guide him away from danger. He'd be safe if he stuck with us."

Peter stopped and looked at his friends to see if they understood what he said. They all nodded and smiled. He continued to walk and speak, "So when Jesus mentioned for the second time that he might be killed, we'd talked about it among ourselves and were confident we knew what was best for him. We'd protect him, and when we reached Jerusalem he'd be acclaimed king and get his priorities right. His miracles would bring us all fame and power in his administration.

"It was soon after Jesus, James, John, and I experienced the presence of heaven's heroes — Moses and Elijah right there with us on the hill, and Jesus shining like the sun, the cloud creeping over us, and God's very voice from heaven. We knew well that God had chosen him and nothing could stop him. We thought he was underrating himself, thinking he'd never succeed against the religious leaders, let alone against Rome. We were sure that with Jesus no one could stop our great cause. We assumed he felt let down after such an exalting experience on the hill. Great people often have swings of mood. He'd get over it. In the next village the needs there would snap him out of it. His compassion always lifted him to the occasion. He'd feel better after healing a few people.

"Jesus didn't quite see the potential we saw," Peter said with a deep breath. He and his students were climbing a street now. They gathered closer around him. "And that day he asked one of those questions we always wanted to dodge. We were back to our headquarters in Capernaum. We gathered in the house and he gave us all reason to avoid meeting his gaze. He said, 'What were you arguing about on the way?' Every one of us, I'm sure, immediately thought of saying, 'Nothing,' but we'd been with him long enough to know we couldn't get away with lying. He'd look us in the face and know immediately if we told the truth. So we didn't answer. Because," Peter stopped and put his hand over his eyes for a moment as he spoke, "I'm ashamed to say that on the road home we twelve had been arguing among ourselves about which of us was the best of Jesus' apprentices.

"We were in for it then. Jesus sat down, summoned us together and said, 'Whoever wants to be first must be last of all and servant of all.' He motioned for us to stay where we were and he went out the door. Soon he was back carrying the neighbors' girl, maybe three years old. Jesus held her there in his arms in the middle of us, turning around so we all saw the kid. He said, 'Whoever welcomes one such child in my name welcomes me, and whoever welcomes me welcomes not me but the one who sent me.' "

Peter and his students had arrived at the villa where he was lodging. Many people awaited him inside. Peter turned to his followers before he entered. He stood silently for a moment, looking in their faces. He spoke slowly, "You all understand, don't you, that neither my being close to Jesus nor your being near to me buys you privileges?"

They said, "Yes."

"Jesus summons us," Peter said, "not to serve our own cause or to live for our own benefit, but to glorify God." Peter looked at each of their faces as they agreed. "Of course you do," he said with a sigh; and, as he entered the villa, his students jostled one another to enter with him.

Discussion Questions

1. What immediate responses do you have to the story?

2. Do you identify with a character in the story? If yes, how and why do you identify with the person? If no, why don't you identify with anyone in the story?

3. Would you like to have a conversation with a character in the story? What would you say, ask, or suggest to the person? Why?

4. How does the story bring the biblical text into a clearer focus for you?

5. How would you improve or modify the story? Why?

6. Most Christians aren't as crass as Jesus' (and Peter's) disciples in seeking or claiming religious priority over others. What are the more subtle ways that we modern disciples seek precedence over other Christians?

7. As a Christian where and when are you most tempted to compare yourself favorably against others?

8. What makes religious people want to be better than others? How can such a desire be transformed into something positive?

9. What further depths of meaning, symbols, connections with, or applications of the biblical faith do you find in the story?

10. Since Jesus Christ has risen from the dead and is alive among us through his Holy Spirit, what of this story would you like Christ to activate in your life?

Chapter 14

Gravensteins

Mark 12:28-34

He could smell them, almost see them in a bucket sitting at the foot of the ladder. He loved Gravenstein apples. That's why he planted the tree fifteen years ago. Now the tree was producing wonderfully, filling the late summer wind with the smell of its sugar; but, Bert was on the wrong side of the seven-foot board fence. The tree stood now in Eve's backyard — Eve, his ex-wife. All he had in his backyard was a peach tree, dripping with late fruit. Peaches made the inside of his mouth break out with sores, so even their smell made him a little sick.

How he loved Gravensteins. As an only child he did everything with his mother — a single parent — from picking the apples, to peeling them, to squashing them through the colander. His mother said, "Would you like a taste?"

Bert, nearly salivating into the bowl, answered, "Yes, please." His mother gave him a spoonful. He closed his eyes as he swallowed and always said, "Mmmm, thank you. You want a bite?"

His mother answered, "Yes, please." His spoonful to her automatically brought the required, "Thank you, would you like a bite?" They ate their fill of Gravenstein applesauce a spoon to one another at a time.

Gravenstein applesauce was the best applesauce on the planet. That's all he could think about every afternoon when he came home from work and walked into his high fenced backyard. Over the fence he saw the top of the ladder against the tree. Eve surely thought of him when she set the ladder up. She must remember he loved that tree. His side of the barricaded yard offered only mouth-destroying peaches.

The divorce had been as civil as possible. The children were grown and married. The finances were simple. All they really owned was the duplex, one side of which they lived in and the other they rented out. The mediator made the obvious suggestion. If they didn't want to sell, they should evict the tenant, then one of them live in one side and one in the other. It was logical. It was economical. It was stupid, Bert thought. But he nodded his head yes, signed the papers, and three weeks later Bert Junior helped him move his things from the small apartment he was renting over a drugstore into the empty side of the duplex. There he began living as his ex-wife's neighbor.

Because they would live so close, he decided in advance how to behave when they met. The wisest course would be never to talk. If they didn't talk, they wouldn't argue. For seven months, the arrangement worked. They saw one another a few times; but, when Bert walked by without speaking, Eve adopted the same pattern.

Now the Gravensteins — in the spring he smelled the blossoms constantly. Then as the fruit set on he walked out of the house into the backyard and stepped backward from Eve's fence to see higher and higher up the tree. Those fruit were beautiful, but they made him feel as lonely as an only child on an empty playground.

He heard a door open on the other side of the fence. Rustling sounds filtered through the fence as Eve walked from her backdoor to somewhere near the tree. He froze. For a few moments he forgot to breathe. He tried to see her movements through the tight slats. He was unprepared to hear her voice.

"Bert," Eve spoke from her side of the fence. He wasn't sure where Eve stood in her yard. He tried to spot movement through the fence's tiny cracks. "Bert," she spoke louder. "I know you're there." He'd heard that tone for over thirty years. It always angered him. "Bert, I'm picking apples. You want some?" He breathed fast now. She was shuffling the ladder and he saw the top lowered, knocking a couple apples off. When he heard them bounce on the sidewalk he answered almost in a whisper, "Yes, please."

"Did you say something?"

"Yes, please," he said a little louder.

"All right. Pick all you want. Just make sure you shut the back gate so Iris doesn't get out. She ran away last week. Okay?"

Bert's thoughts seemed mashed together like apples in a colander. He spoke almost automatically, "Thank you." Through a couple cracks in the fence he thought he saw her move. By the sound he pictured her dragging the ladder toward the house. Almost in spite of himself he said, "Eve?"

"Yes."

"You want some peaches?"

"Sure. Thanks."

"Yeah," Bert said, swallowing hard, "thank *you*."

Discussion Questions

1. What immediate responses do you have to the story?

2. Do you identify with a character in the story? If yes, how and why do you identify with the person? If no, why don't you identify with anyone in the story?

3. Would you like to have a conversation with a character in the story? What would you say, ask, or suggest to the person? Why?

4. How does the story bring the biblical text into a clearer focus for you?

5. How would you improve or modify the story? Why?

6. When have you felt the sting of the command to love your neighbor?

7. Have you experienced estranged neighbors settling a problem amiably?

8. Why is one's neighbor so difficult to love?

9. What further depths of meaning, symbols, connections with, or applications of the biblical faith do you find in the story?

10. Since Jesus Christ has risen from the dead and is alive among us through his Holy Spirit, what of this story would you like Christ to activate in your life?

Emphasis or special occasion: Resurrection Sunday

Chapter 15

Collision Course To The Cross

Mark 15:21-26

Note 1: If reading this story out loud to a group, something like the following needs to be included in the worship before this story:

Leader: Since the earliest days of the faith, it has been appropriate and expected that Christians greet one another on Easter morning: The Lord has risen!
People: He has risen indeed.

Note 2: Pause at each * * * in order to allow listeners to make the switch from scene to scene. Or, have two people read: one narrating for Simon and the other for Jesus. The reader will need to make a distinction between reading narration and the first-person narratives.

* * *

Simon of Cyrene limped through Jerusalem's giant gate. He was muttering. *I can't blame anyone else. It was my idea from beginning to end. I moved my family here.*

He passed through the thick wall into the capital of his faith. *I struggled against my parents, brother, and sisters. I bullied my wife and contradicted her family. I commanded my sons. So we're stuck in Jerusalem and it's my fault.*

He smelled the camels before he saw them. As he shuffled through the bazaar on his bad ankle, people around him waved their arms, shouting at one another, some grunted, some added sighs to their haggling. This marketplace was not very different than where he'd conducted business daily in Cyrene. That, although only half a year before, now seemed a lifetime ago.

* * *

Earlier in the day, on the other side of Jerusalem, the chief priests held a consultation with the elders and scribes and the whole council. They bound Jesus the Galilean, led him away, and handed him over to the prefect Pilate. Pilate interrogated him, "Are you the King of the Jews?" Jesus answered him, "You say so." Then the chief priests accused Jesus of many things. Pilate asked him again, "Have you no answer? See how many charges they bring against you." Jesus made no further reply, so that Pilate was amazed.

* * *

As he walked, Simon clasped his hands tightly behind him in order to endure the pain of his left ankle. *I'm sure it was listening to the psalms. That's what did it: The psalms. I heard them all my life, chanted them as I walked, repeated them as I worked. They praised God's holy Jerusalem. They extolled Zion's tiny hill.*

We dwelt healthily and happily in Cyrene — pleasant ocean breeze, trained and faithful employees in my honey business, a thriving synagogue group to worship with. But I reasoned that if it was that good to be a Judean in a foreign land, it must be better in Jerusalem itself — living finally in the city we sang about. Now my family's in a tumult, Sappira longing for her home and angry at me. Our sons, Alexander and Rufus, with no friends. Every synagogue group we worship with is busy arguing, and the closer to Passover, the worse the bickering becomes.

Jerusalem's Judeans restrict their thinking to one cause. They either want to kill all the Romans, sell out to the Romans completely, or flee to the wilderness to await messiahs who will solve all their problems. They can't seem to get along. Judeans outside our homeland in Cyrene appreciated seeing one another. Sure we had our disagreements, but we banded together against any opposition.

Simon stumbled upon his shaky left ankle through Jerusalem's narrow streets. In some places Passover pilgrims so enlarged the throng that he had to turn sideways to edge into an alley.

* * *

Not far away, because it was the Passover, the prefect Pilate would release a prisoner, anyone for whom the crowd asked. A man named Barabbas was in prison with other the rebels who committed murder during the insurrection. So the crowd came and began to ask Pilate to do for them according to his custom. Pilate answered, "Do you want me to release for you the King of the Jews?" He realized that the chief priests handed Jesus over because of their jealousy. But the chief priests stirred up the crowd to have him release Barabbas for them. Pilate spoke to them again, "Then what do you wish me to do with the man you call the King of the Jews?" They shouted back, "Crucify him!" Pilate asked them, "Why, what evil has he done?" They shouted all the more, "Crucify him!" So Pilate, wishing to satisfy the crowd, released Barabbas for them; and after flogging Jesus, he handed him over to be crucified.

* * *

Simon stepped aside for four men to pass. Their robes were shorter than Judeans wore. He caught the Latin words for "large" and "temple." He could tell by their pointing and wide-eyed staring that they were pilgrims visiting Jerusalem for Passover.

What can I do with Alexander and Rufus, such lethargic sons? I can't allow them just to hop on a boat by themselves and sail a month back to their old home. Sappira wouldn't allow it either. Yet they're so irritable and surly, fighting with each other and me. Since this ankle gave out again, it's impossible for me to labor a whole day. But I almost have to beat the boys to get them to work.

If I hadn't sunk our money into this house and field, if I'd just brought the family on a visit to Jerusalem to see what it's like, try it out. Or, I could've asked friends what it's like for foreign-born Judeans to return to the mother city. Instead, I dragged Sappira and the boys from the only place they knew. I still see her tears and hear her weeping as our boat caught the evening's wind in Apollonia's harbor, our families ashore waving, my father stamping his foot, leaving the others, and turning back toward Cyrene.

* * *

The soldiers led Jesus into the courtyard of the governor's headquarters. They called together the whole cohort. They clothed Jesus in a purple cloak, and after twisting some thorns into a crown, they put it on him. They began saluting him, "Hail, King of the Jews!" They struck his head with a reed, spat upon him, and knelt down in homage to him. After mocking him, they stripped him of the purple cloak and put his own clothes on him. Then they led him out to crucify him.

* * *

I've got to find a way out of this mess, Simon thought, and soon. I don't want the children to push me around. I can't admit to Sappira I've made a mistake. And if I'd sail into Apollonia and stagger up to Cyrene, I'd have to find work or start a business. I'd do so with an empty money box and a gimpy leg. When old Jason bought my swarms of honeybees, he laughed. "You'll regret this. Why move to Jerusalem? You'll find Rome's soldiers in every city. How different can one city be from another? Besides, people make pilgrimage to this holy city, too."

Simon was nearing his house. *If I bundle up the family and return to Cyrene, I'll have to acknowledge to my father, and more humiliating, to my father-in-law, that I made a ruinous mistake. I'll be the town buffoon. For the rest of my life I'll hear people use my name as a by-word for leaping before I looked, for letting faith get in the way of careful planning. That's what it was. This is all because I had great ideas about God and what God was going to do for us in Jerusalem. God,* Simon prayed as he walked, *why am I here? Can't you do your work anywhere? Am I supposed to do something for you here that I couldn't do in Cyrene?* He turned a corner and saw a Roman execution squad clumped around a criminal crumpled in the street. The man lay under the beam that would be his cross' horizontal bar. Thorns encircled his head. His face was in a mud puddle.

* * *

The report, written more than a generation later, put it this way: "They compelled a passer-by, who was coming in from the country, to carry Jesus' cross; it was Simon of Cyrene, the father of Alexander and Rufus. Then they brought Jesus to the place called Golgotha (which means the place of a skull). They offered him wine mixed with myrrh; but he did not take it. They crucified him, and divided his clothes among them, casting lots to decide what each should take. It was nine o'clock in the morning when they crucified him. The inscription of the charge against him read, 'The King of the Jews.'"

* * *

Simon, despite the sorriest blunder of his life, and despite all his confusion, pain, and disappointment, was where God could use him. When he found himself surrounded by soldiers and then carrying the crossbeam upon which Jesus would die, he forgot his own, minor problems and even some of the ache surging from the sole of his left foot to his knee. His carrying Jesus' cross set a new course for him and his family. His family's life was changed so much by meeting Jesus that more than thirty years later the name of Simon of Cyrene and his sons Alexander and Rufus were included in the gospel record.

We, too, might not have known that Jesus has been approaching us; but God surprises us with Jesus' cross, no matter if we are burdened with concerns for our family or business, for our health, neighbors, or nation. We have only to turn a corner to find that Jesus' life and death intersects our lives right where we live, whether or not we're satisfied with ourselves or where we live.

Jesus meets each of us in this world. He seems surprisingly weak and in need of our help. But when we heft Jesus' cross and feel it cut into our shoulder, we find, as did Simon of Cyrene, that Jesus rearranges our plans, tosses our priorities into a new pattern, renews our minds, and grants new birth to our spirits. We're given better things to concentrate our thoughts and efforts upon than where we should live, what we'd like to own, or what others will think of us.

For the sake of our Lord Jesus we now lug his cross into our world until finally, when nothing seems worse and when we see no hope or way out of ours or the world's problems, whether two days, two years, or two millennia later, Jesus surprises us with a resurrection.

Leader: The Lord has risen.
People: He has risen indeed!
Leader: The Lord has risen.
People: He has risen indeed!

Discussion Questions

1. What immediate responses do you have to the story?

2. Do you identify with a character in the story? If yes, how and why do you identify with the person? If no, why don't you identify with anyone in the story?

3. Would you like to have a conversation with a character in the story? What would you say, ask, or suggest to the person? Why?

4. How does the story bring the biblical text into a clearer focus for you?

5. How would you improve or modify the story? Why?

6. Have you been disillusioned of the hope that a new place to live would change your life for the better?

7. Have you been surprised by an encounter with Jesus? How has even your suffering seemed to lead you to meet Jesus?

8. What does it mean for you to carry your cross as Jesus' follower?

9. What further depths of meaning, symbols, connections with, or applications of the biblical faith do you find in the story?

10. Since Jesus Christ has risen from the dead and is alive among us through his Holy Spirit, what of this story would you like Christ to activate in your life?

Chapter 16

Rich And Poor Alike?

Luke 6:17-26

Lalia nagged Corin for weeks, "Come to church with me Sunday night. It's wonderful." Corin wasn't against religion. She'd just been busy for her first three years of college. She'd get around to it. But this week, Lalia found the crack to slip the wedge in, "I know you don't have much going this Monday. My Volkswagen's fixed. So how about if we go to church Sunday night?"

"Okay," Corin said, without thinking about what she was agreeing to.

Lalia smiled broadly. Corin gave a half smile. "You'll love it," Lalia said. "I know you will."

Corin had the ability to think place by place and subject by subject without blurring the edges. When she studied biology, nothing else entered her mind. When she scrubbed tables at the student union, she never thought of schoolwork. Consequently, although she agreed to worship and hadn't forgotten it, on Sunday evening she was surprised when Lalia lifted her attention from her chemistry book saying, "Time for worship."

As they approached in Lalia's car, the church surprised her more. She heard it was large, but she simply multiplied her parents' church times four. However, Pastor Harvey's Worship Center was as big as a warehouse with a campus that seemed as large as her college.

On the shuttle bus from the distant parking lot Lalia perceived Corin's apprehension. She said, "You'll love Pastor Harvey."

After they navigated through the entry with its coffee kiosk, bookstore, and T-shirt shop, they stepped into the sanctuary. Corin gasped so loudly that a teenage boy near turned to her and chuckled. The auditorium could have held a basketball stadium. Opposite her she saw four students from her college wearing their colors of black and orange. They were so far away that, as they shuffled through the plush, green seats, they looked like a caterpillar on a leaf.

An orchestra played. Projected images illumined three colossal screens. Ushers circulated, offering brochures about Pastor Harvey's DVDs and advertising the congregation's seminars. In the middle of the stage, a man with carefully groomed blond hair stepped up to lead the singing group of a dozen young and handsome men and women who glided down from the choir. Corin calculated that the choir was as large as her parents' congregation.

The lights slowly dimmed on the congregation. The worship minister welcomed all and began to lead them in songs that seemed to Corin like those at their college pep rallies. Only this was better. The sound seemed to enter Corin from every direction. Thirteen thousand, maybe 14,000 people singing praise to God. It continued for 45 minutes. She was swept away by it, feeling herself moved, uplifted, shaken. In the pause after the last song she tried to compare it with anything she'd before experienced. She couldn't. No category she could name would fit this worship. It was the greatest thing she ever experienced — until Pastor Harvey preached.

After worship, as Corin walked out through the happy crowd, Lalia looked at her with an upturned twist of her head that meant: Well, what do you think now? Corin said, "We don't have to take the shuttle to the car. I'll just float there." Lalia hugged her and their giggling in the shuttle didn't bother anyone. Everyone was happy.

All the next day, no matter what Corin concentrated on — chemistry lab, anatomy, or even during psychology class — Sunday night's worship seeped into her consciousness. She heard Pastor Harvey's repeating, "You're a child of God. God wants the best for you. Pray for the best." When she remembered his long prayer, she thought of the debts she was accruing in college. She never considered that because she was God's child she should pray for a high paying job with good benefits — as well as a nice house and new car.

During the week, she and Lalia talked often about the worship center. There was no question whether they'd attend next Sunday — until Thursday evening. Their phone rang. Lalia got it and mostly listened for two minutes, answering, "Yes ... Sure I will ... I can be there tomorrow night by eleven." It was her brother, asking her to watch his two children for the weekend as his wife recovered from surgery.

Corin was now without transportation to worship. For the first time in her life, she was eager to get to worship. She asked a few people who had cars, but found no one going to worship, at least not to the worship center.

In chemistry class on Friday afternoon, she asked her lab partner, Kenny. He said, "I've got a car, but why don't you come to my church on Sunday." This was her last chance and it would be impolite to insist on his worshiping where she wanted. She said, "Okay."

Sunday morning, 11 a.m. The songs were older, slower hymns. Worship wasn't necessarily joyful. Quiet, reverent, yes, but not moving. The pastor was a middle-aged woman, prematurely gray: Lena Jurry. The text for the sixth Sunday of Epiphany was Jesus' teaching in Luke 6:17-26.

The pastor encouraged worshipers to bring staples for the food bank every Sunday. She urged them to join in building a Habitat for Humanity house. She directed them to sign a petition to the state legislature to raise the minimum wage. Especially, Pastor Jurry emphasized Jesus' saying, "Blessed are you who are poor, for yours is the kingdom of God," and "But woe to you who are rich, for you have received your consolation."

Corin was courteous to Kenny after worship but declined his offer of lunch. She needed to think and she needed to think hard; because in her mind the two churches weren't coming together. She couldn't find enough similarities to fit them into one group. Were they even the same religion?

Discussion Questions

1. What immediate responses do you have to the story?

2. Do you identify with a character in the story? If yes, how and why do you identify with the person? If no, why don't you identify with anyone in the story?

3. Would you like to have a conversation with a character in the story? What would you say, ask, or suggest to the person? Why?

4. How does the story bring the biblical text into a clearer focus for you?

5. How would you improve or modify the story? Why?

6. Of the two kinds of worship Corin experienced, which is closer to the worship you are used to or that you are drawn to?

7. How would you prepare someone to come to worship for the first time in your home church?

8. If you were to design the perfect worship service, what would it be? Why? How would it honor the full biblical revelation and not just a narrow selection from Jesus' ministry?

9. What further depths of meaning, symbols, connections with, or applications of the biblical faith do you find in the story?

10. Since Jesus Christ has risen from the dead and is alive among us through his Holy Spirit, what of this story would you like Christ to activate in your life?

Chapter 17

Signs

Luke 21:25-36

"Cres, I've got to talk to you," was all that could be heard over this newfangled marvel named the "telephone." Connections were poor in Winnemucca, Nevada, in 1915. Alice couldn't even raise Central Exchange to be reconnected. But Alice heard clearly enough, "Cres, I've got to talk to you." Even if Alice hadn't recognized the tinny voice, she knew who it was. No matter that her last name had been Venneman for 23 years, the former Alice Creswell was always "Cres" to Peg Reed.

"I'm going over to Peg's," Alice yelled to Ernest. "Sounds like she's upset."

"Want a ride?" Ernest said, sticking his head into the hall from the den. "The car's working. Paper said ash is bad for the lungs."

"I'll wear my hat and tie a scarf around my face. I'll be okay."

Outside, Alice encountered a gray world. The late May air appeared to be snowing, but it wasn't cold. Even the moon was obscured by the blinding clouds of ash. She occasionally blinked an ash from her eye as she walked along anticipating Peg's anxiety. Lately Peg was more nervous than usual. Probably the ash. But, if Peg didn't have something to worry about, she'd actively seek it.

In high school, Alice and Peg were neighbors in the small, tough frontier town. Alice and Peg clung together as much in mutual defense as in affection. But twelve years ago, Peg took an acute turn when she was rounded up by an end-of-the-world group. Since then, Peg lost the ability to plan or organize her life, which had never been easy for her. She usually had a job, but never made much money. If she hadn't lived with her elderly father to care for him, she couldn't survive financially.

At the Reeds' house, the perimeter of the porch's floor was white with ash as with a light dusting of snow. Alice stepped under its roof, shook like a dog, and snapped her scarf clean. She shook out her hair as she knocked on the door.

"Cres," Peg opened the door with wide eyes. "Get in here."

"What's up, Peg?" Alice asked as she stepped in, still brushing herself off.

"It's the end," Peg said. "I figured it out." She grabbed Alice's hands excitedly in her own. "The war in Europe. Mount Lassen erupting. It's been a year of both."

"The end?"

"The end of the world, Cres. It's gotta' be. Nothing like this before."

"I thought you were off that. I thought those folks left town when the world didn't end."

Peg spoke louder, "Bishop and Mrs. Hyde were near to being right. When you calculate 2,000 years, to be off by only a dozen is pretty close."

Alice slapped some ash off her knee. "How's Mr. Reed?"

"He's good tonight," Peg said. "He's sitting at the window like it's snowing. He lit a fire in the fireplace. Said it matched the mood."

"Let's hear what he thinks," Alice said.

Mr. Reed was seated in a large chair. "Daddy, Cres is here," Peg said.

He replaced a book in the bookcase next to him and said, "Hi, Alice." He'd taught Alice science in high school. "What you think of this hard snow?"

"We'll see if Ernest gets his Model-T stuck in it as quickly as he gets it stuck in real snow," Alice said.

Mr. Reed laughed. He pointed out the window. "Pretty exciting, isn't it? The old earth spitting up like a baby?"

"Daddy," Peg said, "It's more than that." She spoke slower and lowered her head slightly, "I think they're signs of the end of the world." Mr. Reed frowned and she spoke quieter, as if answering him, "You know — the moon and stars darkened and the war across Europe."

Mr. Reed and Alice looked at one another. They'd dealt with Peg's various worries before. "What about you, Alice?" He asked with the tone of prepping a student for a text. "You think the world's ending?"

"Well," Alice said, "I don't know —"

"The world's always ending, and always beginning," he said when she answered too slowly. "Volcanoes have burst forth for millennia. If they don't crush the land with lava or mudflows, like old Mount Lassen's trying to do, they give us a lot of sand to sweep off Winnemucca's roofs. And the spring grass," he motioned out the window to their dark yard, "that's coated tonight with ash will push up and grow green tomorrow."

"That's just nature, Daddy," Peg said. "I think God's going to end it."

Mr. Reed leaned back in his chair. Alice knew that he hadn't agreed with Bishop and Mrs. Hyde, but he was kind to them, and Peg had been faithful to him. Even though she worshiped in the Bishop's tabernacle, she walked her father to the Methodist church for worship every Sunday and arranged for someone to accompany him home.

"Honey," he said to Peg. "The world will to end someday. But people who predict *when* are always wrong. God'll come up with a new world, or kingdom, or whatever God wants to call it. But God's not going to abandon us. Keep your head up and live for God no matter what."

Peg seemed ready to cry. Mr. Reed reached over and rubbed her hand. "It looks bad around the world tonight, but there's been worse. Time'll probably come when things seem worse than 1915. Stand tall and live for God, and let's see what tomorrow brings." He smiled at Peg and Alice, raising and lowering his shoulders with a sigh, meaning class was dismissed.

Alice and Peg drank tea in the kitchen until Peg seemed calm enough for Alice to leave. Alice walked home through a particularly heavy ash fall. In the past she hadn't thought much about the world ending. She brushed ash from her hat and tried to walk with her head high as she prayed that Mr. Reed was right.

Discussion Questions

1. What immediate responses do you have to the story?

2. Do you identify with a character in the story? If yes, how and why do you identify with the person? If no, why don't you identify with anyone in the story?

3. Would you like to have a conversation with a character in the story? What would you say, ask, or suggest to the person? Why?

4. How does the story bring the biblical text into a clearer focus for you?

5. How would you improve or modify the story? Why?

6. Have you been around people obsessed with the end of the world? What's it like to be with them?

7. What are your biggest fears about the world?

8. Do you think much about the end of the world? What heightens or increases this subject's coming to your mind?

9. What further depths of meaning, symbols, connections with, or applications of the biblical faith do you find in the story?

10. Since Jesus Christ has risen from the dead and is alive among us through his Holy Spirit, what of this story would you like Christ to activate in your life?

Emphasis or special occasion: Maundy (Holy) Thursday or Good Friday

Chapter 18

Third Voice In The Courtyard

Luke 22:54-66

The day is so pleasant: warm with a gentle breeze rippling the grass nearby. Why is Nehorai, the steward, yelling loudly to Yodan? This garden's spreading trees offer shade and ripe fruit. Yodan is most pleased to lie beside the trickling stream that feeds the glassy pool. Why is Nehorai so frenzied, calling to Yodan even louder? Yodan relaxes while all his fellow slaves line up to serve him. Now Nehorai screeches not only to Yodan but to each slave by name.

Yodan opened his eyes. Nehorai shook him violently and screamed in his face, "Wake up, you stupid slave, and make the courtyard ready for the council."

As Yodan sat up, his cloak fell to the ground and he felt the cold. Nehorai pulled the other slaves by the hair or kicked them from their coverings. Yodan stood up, stretching with a great yawn. "It's the middle of the night." He stared at the steward as though he were moonstruck. "What do you mean, 'prepare for the council'?"

Nehorai charged at him, aiming his fist toward Yodan's face. "No questions, imbecile. They're bringing a prisoner for interrogation. This courtyard's a mess."

Yodan looked upon the courtyard and he almost leaped out of his clothes. Last night he left the other slaves and trusted them to clean up after the late Passover celebration. They hadn't. Dirty dishes, cushions, and baskets laid around the courtyard and, nearest to Caiaphas' quarters, he could make out in the moon's dim light a couple large pottery jars broken into pieces.

Yodan heard voices, people coming down the street. He saw the glow of their torches over the courtyard wall. He grasped his cloak, ran, and threw it on the ground beside the broken pottery. In the moonlight's shadows his hands were a gray blur of movement, tossing shards onto the cloak. Both hands, scooping and picking up. He was barely aware of his fellow slaves also scrambling to straighten up the courtyard. He worked so fast in the darkness that almost every movement cut his hands. Finally, as swiftly as he could, he slid his hands, palms flat, back and forth over the flagstones like two fast, giant spiders, trying methodically to feel the ground for even the smallest piece. He quickly wrapped the cloak around the shards and was running across the courtyard as the crowd plunged loudly through the gateway.

The mob rushed in from Yodan's left. Caiaphas and his attendants entered from his right. Yodan ducked as he ran between them, wishing he were invisible. Halfway across the courtyard he saw other slaves dashing out of the way.

As the crowd entered with their torches, and as slaves set large-wicked lamps onto stands in the courtyard, Yodan looked around to see if any evidence remained of his negligence. Nehorai, the steward, had granted him the privilege of celebrating the Passover in the courtyard with his fellow slaves. They could do so only after Caiaphas and his family retired for the night. It was a special privilege granted to the high priest's slaves. Yodan had promised, "to leave the area as though it had never been used." He stayed awake too late, became too tired, and he was a fool to trust the two slaves who swore they'd clean up. They were from Damascus. He shouldn't have trusted Syrian slaves.

"Uh oh," Semqah said, quietly. Yodan was so absorbed in the courtyard's happenings he hadn't noticed Semqah beside him. "You know who that is?" Semqah whispered, pointing to the soldiers and their prisoner.

"Well, isn't it...?" Yodan squinted in the dark as he wiped his bleeding hands on his cloak. "Yes, the Galilean. He didn't last long did he?"

"King-for-a-week Jesus," Semqah whispered. "I knew, with people tossing branches and cloaks and shouting 'king,' it wouldn't take long before old Joseph Caiaphas got him."

Yodan and Semqah watched one group of soldiers hold torches, while another group kicked and pushed the prisoner.

"Fine way to celebrate Passover's freedom," Semqah whispered. "Makes all the high-sounding ceremony last night seem pointless."

"Bring the prisoner," Caiaphas shouted, summoning the group past the low wall and toward his quarters. Jesus was shoved toward Caiaphas and the other council members, as slaves brought stubby braziers to their sides to warm them. Nehorai spoke to each cluster of slaves that squatted in the dark at the edges of the courtyard, telling them to stay quiet, awake, and out of the way. No one knew how long this interrogation would last, but everyone must remain alert until it was finished. After a while one slave brought burning sticks to the center of the courtyard and others carried dry wood. Soon a good fire was burning. Semqah and Yodan began to move toward the fire when Semqah nudged Yodan, "Look who's here."

Yodan followed Semqah's gaze to the courtyard entrance. A man stood in the shadows for a moment, speaking to the doorkeeper who nodded and waved him in. The man seemed to creep in, glancing around apprehensively.

"That's their second in command," Semqah said, his hand concealing his lips. "Name's Peter."

Yodan and Semqah moved slowly toward the fire. Neither wanted to draw attention to himself. Yodan was still scrutinizing the courtyard to make sure all was clean. He was gaping over the low partition at the backs of those who surrounded Jesus. As he walked, he gazed at the ground beside Caiaphas. For a moment, as he extended his neck to the left, he thought he saw through the legs of soldiers something lying near the high priest's feet. He slowed but continued to shuffle toward the fire, trying from twenty paces away to inspect the flagstones beneath Caiaphas' feet.

With the slaves mumbling near the fire, it was hard to hear what the priests, soldiers, and prisoner were saying. Someone beside Jesus yelled, "Liar!" The slaves at the fire turned to see what was going on, but nothing much could be seen. Yodan used the distraction to look more carefully, trying to peer over the partition to determine if any sign of his irresponsibility laid near the chief priest's feet.

"I don't see why they're making such a pretense of justice," Semqah said, speaking quietly out the side of his mouth. "They're just keeping us all awake. They're going to kill him."

Yodan was almost standing on tiptoes as he stretched his neck, first leaning right then left, yet trying to appear casual. One of the women slaves had been staring at Peter. She pointed to him. "This man also was with him."

Peter, holding out his hand shushed her, "Woman, I do not know him."

Yodan looked at the council members around Jesus. A couple of them turned to see what the commotion was with the slaves.

"Quiet," Yodan said. "We'll all get flogged."

He stepped a pace to the side and with that movement in the light of the lamps, torches, and braziers, he saw a large shard of a jar right beside Caiaphas' sandal. He gasped so hard he almost swallowed his tongue. He felt the skin tighten all over his body. If Caiaphas found out about the late celebration in the courtyard, it made no difference if it were Passover, Yodan would be pulling an oar on a Roman grain ship until he died.

Priests clustered around the prisoner. For a minute Caiaphas' face was obscured by the back of Jesus' head. Yodan watched intently, wondering how he could keep Caiaphas from noticing the shard or how he could retrieve it without being detected. Just then, one of the other slaves at the fire said to Peter, "You also are one of them."

In a loud voice Peter said, "Man, I am not!"

At that, the discussion among the council members halted for a moment, as they looked toward the slaves warming themselves at the fire. Caiaphas frowned, turned to Nehorai, and sent him over with a shake of his head.

Nehorai charged the group and they all quickly stood. Nehorai hesitated, sucking in his breath, frightening them all the more by the pause before speaking. "You mindless fools." He spoke quietly and rhythmically through his clenched teeth, "The next idiot to disturb these proceedings will be whipped. Male *or* female," he said.

When Nehorai left, Peter abandoned the fire and for about an hour he leaned against one of the courtyard's outer pillars, speaking to no one. Yodan also remained standing. He could tell they were finishing with Jesus and were about to send him away, kill him somehow. The moon was setting. The eastern sky began to show the faintest pink.

Peter had just returned to the circle around the fire, when Yodan saw Caiaphas kick something with his foot and look down to see what it was. Immediately Yodan pointed across the fire to Peter and yelled as loudly as he could, "Surely this man also was with him; for he is a Galilean."

Peter looked at him with surprise and fear, "Man, I do not know what you are talking about!"

When the priests and soldiers turned to see who had been accused and who was denying it so loudly, Yodan shouted again, "Surely this man also was with him; for he is a Galilean." At that moment a rooster crowed. Jesus for the first time turned toward the courtyard and looked directly at his companion by the fire, who appeared dazed and guilt-stricken. Three soldiers started for him, but he dashed from the courtyard. He began weeping as he left and his bitter cries echoed down the street as he fled. The slaves were puzzled. One shrugged and sniggered. But they were too tired to guess what Peter's leaving might mean.

The remaining soldiers seemed to leap at once upon Jesus. They blindfolded him, beat, and mocked him. In the uproar, Yodan slipped along the side of the courtyard to where Caiaphas had stood. Caiaphas was only a few paces away, being turned toward the battering and mocking of the blindfolded prisoner. He commanded Jesus to prophesy and tell who had hit him. Council members were milling around, taunting him. Yodan spied the shard, took two paces behind Caiaphas, stooped, and grabbed it. No sooner had he stuffed it under his cloak than Caiaphas spun toward him. For three fast heartbeats Caiaphas looked at Yodan. Caiaphas had huge, shaggy eyebrows that made his eyes seem to recede into caves. He peered at the fresh blood on Yodan's cloak. Whenever before Caiaphas had stared at Yodan, Yodan always ended up being punished. Caiaphas looked down and seemed to search for something. Yodan did his best to appear innocent.

At daybreak, they took Jesus away. The slaves sought places to lie down and sleep. Even the gatekeeper was asleep, sitting back against the door. Yodan stood momentarily at the burned-out fire and looked around. He was exhausted. His hands were aching with cuts. Blood stained his palms, but he was exultant. There aren't many times you can escape so completely and somebody else takes the blame.

Yodan laid down next to a wall in the sun; but instead of sleeping, when he closed his eyes he saw Peter's expression when accused of being Jesus' follower. He heard a noise and opened his eyes. Caiaphas stood where he'd been during the interrogation. He was searching the courtyard floor. He looked at Yodan. For an instant their eyes met. Caiaphas' deep eyes seemed to peer out of holes in a ragged cliff. He frowned angrily, pulled his cloak around himself, and departed toward his quarters. Suddenly, Yodan knew that somehow, for something, he would be punished. He wished he could get someone else punished for this too, but he had no idea how.

Discussion Questions

1. What immediate responses do you have to the story?

2. Do you identify with a character in the story? If yes, how and why do you identify with the person? If no, why don't you identify with anyone in the story?

3. Would you like to have a conversation with a character in the story? What would you say, ask, or suggest to the person? Why?

4. How does the story bring the biblical text into a clearer focus for you?

5. How would you improve or modify the story? Why?

6. Can you picture in your mind the events of Jesus' trial? What do you think about it and how do you feel when you imagine it?

7. Can you also imagine what went on around Jesus' trial with other people? Which can you imagine better and which makes more of an impact upon you: What occurred in Jesus trial or what occurred around Jesus' trial?

8. How does watching the event of Jesus' interrogation through the "camera" of Yodan's point of view help you understand Jesus' sufferings and Peter's denial? How does it help you reflect upon your own lapses in faith and obedience?

9. What further depths of meaning, symbols, connections with, or applications of the biblical faith do you find in the story?

10. Since Jesus Christ has risen from the dead and is alive among us through his Holy Spirit, what of this story would you like Christ to activate in your life?

Emphasis or special occasion: Resurrection Sunday

Chapter 19

Joseph Of Arimathea And Of Jerusalem

Luke 23:50-56

Note: If reading this story out loud to a group, something like the following needs to be included in the worship before this story:

Leader: Since the earliest days of the faith, it has been appropriate and expected that Christians greet one another on Easter morning: The Lord has risen!
People: **He has risen indeed.**

* * *

"Yes, Mother. Enoch told me the centurion took Father into Pilate's palace."

"Was he being guarded? Was he under arrest?" Huldah asked.

"Enoch said he didn't seem to be. They'd walked into the city from the north. That's where Enoch spotted them and followed. He said, 'It was Joseph of Arimathea. I couldn't believe it. Your father and a Roman centurion, walking solemnly and silently. I stayed twenty paces behind until they entered the palace.' Then Enoch left and went searching for me."

"Phinehas, you've got to go right now and help your father. You can't let him face the Romans alone."

"What could I do? No one can get into the Roman palace tonight, not even a member of the council. And even if they could, you wouldn't find two from all of the council members who'd lift a hand for Father."

Huldah bit her lip as she peered through the window into the moonlit evening.

"But if he's not in trouble with the Romans," Phinehas said, "he'll soon be in trouble with the rest of the council, because the sun's down. He's now violating the sabbath."

"At least the moon's out," she said. "This afternoon when those thick clouds covered the sun, it was black as death. Never seen it so dark. All afternoon I'd suddenly realize I was shivering."

She pulled the cover over the window and turned to her son. "You've got to do something about your father. No, no," she said to her son's gesture of protest. "Not just tonight. He hasn't been thinking well lately. He's been confused."

"Confused about what?"

"At first I thought ... I thought it was because he kept sneaking out to listen to that Galilean teacher, but it's more. He talks of moving back to Arimathea."

"To Arimathea? Oh my! What would he do at his age? They don't need scholars there."

"I know. I tell him. But he complains that he is thirty years a resident of Jerusalem and still known as 'Joseph of Arimathea.' The council had to admit him, since he's more learned than them all, yet he's never felt welcome. Only one friend among them. I told him the first day of last week I thought it was crazy to leave. He wandered out of the house and back to the temple in time to watch the Galilean toss tables around."

"That explains it, then," Phinehas said. "When Father and I were patching the roof a month ago, he straightened his back and stood for a long time looking north toward the olive grove. And out of nowhere he said, 'I think I'll sell the tomb, too.'"

"The tomb?"

"That's what he said," Phinehas answered.

"Oh, no he won't. Just got it finished, and it's for all of us. That's the only lasting way we'll ever be equals to Jerusalem's snooty old families."

Huldah was still enumerating the expenses for hewing the tomb, when Joseph entered, closed the door, and stood pressing his back against it.

Phinehas raised his hands as if in prayer. "Father, where've you been? The sabbath commenced long ago."

"Phinehas' friend, Enoch, said you entered the palace with a Roman centurion," Huldah said. "What were you doing?"

Joseph gazed blankly between them. He walked to the peg on the wall that held the family's menorah. "It needs to be lit," he said, and handed it to his wife.

"Father, we've worried about you. What's kept you out after sunset?"

Joseph picked up a cup near the fire, turned it over and over, slowly drumming his fingers on it, and set it back. He spoke so quietly they barely could hear him. "I've been at the olive grove."

Phinehas said, "What were you doing at the olive grove?"

"I sat. For a long time." He sighed and slouched, bracing against the wall. "By the full moon I looked toward the city and the temple. I peered around at the pilgrims' campfires. I sat in front of the tomb's stone door and thought."

Neither Phinehas nor Huldah spoke. They waited. Joseph bowed his head and said, "The tomb's door is now shut."

They couldn't speak, just stared at him. He looked up to them and answered their unspoken question: "Jesus of Nazareth, executed today, crucified."

"You put someone else in our tomb?" Huldah said. "You wasted a third of our fortune to hew out that hillside and then you put a stranger in it? That was for us and our children and our children's children."

"If he'd hung on the cross after sundown, the land would've been defiled."

"Let the land be defiled," she said. "At least let all of Jerusalem be defiled."

"No. I wouldn't. And besides, I couldn't let them throw him into the common criminals' grave, and I had only a little time from when he died — he died quickly — until he must be in the tomb."

"You didn't have to bury him."

"As I reckoned, it fell to me to bury him. His students didn't come to perform their duty. His family did nothing. Someone had to."

"You put a stranger in our tomb!" Huldah said. "You released the door to roll shut over the entry of my tomb with an executed criminal inside!"

"He wasn't a criminal," Joseph shouted.

"If he wasn't a criminal, he wouldn't have been crucified," Huldah raised her voice.

"It was unjust. He was not —."

"Father! Mother!" Phinehas said as he stepped between them. "Let's figure this out. What exactly happened?"

"But —" Huldah said.

"Mother, wait!" He held his hand up to quiet her. "Father, what happened? From the beginning, why were you with the centurion entering Pilate's palace?"

"That was far from the beginning. It started early this morning. That's why I was roused early. I was summoned to an extraordinary meeting of the council. They tried Jesus of Nazareth for blasphemy. Neither Nicodemus nor I concurred, but they found him guilty anyway." He shook his head and grimaced. "They turned him over to Pilate who finally agreed to crucify him for sedition. By the time they got Pilate to agree, the crowd had pretty well given up on Jesus, and it didn't take much rousing from the councilors to incite them to yell, 'Crucify him!' "

Joseph pushed his hand against his forehead. "I was near when he died. As I said, I waited, but no one came to bury him, so I asked the centurion for permission. He took me to Pilate. He was amazed Jesus died so soon; but he granted me the corpse. When I went back to Golgotha to get Jesus' body, Nicodemus was there. All he said was, 'Need help?' "

"We got him down and wrapped him in the shroud, and I didn't think twice about putting him in our tomb. It was the right thing to do, no matter the cost. Jesus was a good and righteous man. I thought God's government would begin with him."

Phinehas put his arm around his mother and both looked at Joseph, waiting for him to tell the rest.

"It was pathetic at the end. No family or students to help, just Nicodemus and I. A bunch of the Galilean women followed us and saw where we put him. Then Nicodemus left and I just sat there as the sun went down, and the earth cooled and quieted, and the Roman guards came. They didn't bother with me. Nothing else I can do now, but I could've done more earlier. I didn't agree with the council's decision, but I didn't disagree very loudly. And councillors were there when Nicodemus and I took him down. By our doing that they understand how much we sympathized with him."

"You think the council will take revenge on you?" Phinehas said.

"I wouldn't be surprised."

"It might not be that bad," Huldah said. She grasped both of Joseph's hands and made him look at her as she spoke. "You stay away from those Galileans. They'll be out of the city after the sabbath. Maybe they've fled already. Avoid them. The council might be angry, but they can't touch you if you'll stay clear of those Galileans."

"I don't know what they'll do." Joseph looked away from them. "But I think it's time I leave the council and Jerusalem and return to Arimathea. I don't fit here."

"Father, you won't fit in Arimathea, either. You've been gone three decades. You can't just step in and start life over. You'd be leaving me and Azura and your grandchildren. Bithia and her children especially need you since Andrew died."

Joseph walked stoop-shouldered to the door. He was shaking his head. He slowly opened the door and stood in the doorway. The night air swirled in around his ankles. He looked into the moonlight and talked, but not to his wife and son behind him.

"If God's government wasn't coming through Jesus, how will it ever arrive? I've waited and prayed for God's government to descend to earth. I've studied the scriptures. Have I studied too much and done too little? Have I questioned too frequently and not believed often enough?" He looked in the direction of his olive grove and spoke as if to a living person. "Have I failed when I was most needed? Will the rest of my life be only remembering and regretting what I didn't do?"

Joseph of Arimathea and of Jerusalem: With what faith he has he does what he can, following the law as he knows it; however, the law only instructs him to bury Jesus. He performs a last gracious act for the Galilean, but now he expects only a sad memory of Jesus and problems because of him.

Joseph's story ends before Jesus' resurrection. Joseph of Arimathea either hasn't heard or doesn't believe that Jesus predicted rising from the dead. He has the highest admiration for Jesus, but he doesn't consider that Jesus will live beyond death.

One can honor Jesus' life — as Joseph does — yet have no belief that Jesus will in any way live again. For most modern people, even those who pack churches on resurrection morning, new life never quite gets here. Like Joseph, many people still wait for God to do something.

This Sunday morning, a day and a half after Joseph and Nicodemus bundled Jesus in linen and laid him in a new tomb, isn't about Joseph of Jerusalem or his family. It isn't about Jesus' followers who fled him, denied him, betrayed him, or simply didn't defend him strenuously enough. This morning isn't about Jesus' family or about the Galilean crowd that followed him. It's about God — not a generic God or a composite God, but the God and Father of Jesus Christ, creator of the world and Lord even of life and death.

This morning God's good news comes from beyond our actions and abilities, beyond our expectations and even from beyond our lives. In Jesus God has done what we can never do. God starts life over right where we are. God starts life over for us at the tomb that belonged to Joseph and to his wife and to you and to me. God starts us over where we've buried Jesus and found our hopes confused and our lives unfulfilled. God starts life over for us where we don't understand others and aren't satisfied with ourselves. Now at this tomb a couple mornings later, a few of Jesus' women followers, who saw where he was buried, tiptoe back into Joseph's olive grove, and God's story of eternal love breaks into Joseph's story and breaks into the gospels' stories, and breaks into our story. The Lord has risen.

People: **He has risen indeed.**
Leader: The Lord has risen!
People: **He has risen indeed!**

Discussion Questions

1. What immediate responses do you have to the story?

2. Do you identify with a character in the story? If yes, how and why do you identify with the person? If no, why don't you identify with anyone in the story?

3. Would you like to have a conversation with a character in the story? What would you say, ask, or suggest to the person? Why?

4. How does the story bring the biblical text into a clearer focus for you?

5. How would you improve or modify the story? Why?

6. What do you suppose the people felt and thought as they took Jesus' body from the cross and prepared it for burial?

7. Have you disagreed with your family about your religious commitments, especially financial religious commitments?

8. When and how have you been disillusioned in your faith? When and how has your faith survived the disillusionment?

9. What further depths of meaning, symbols, connections with, or applications of the biblical faith do you find in the story?

10. Since Jesus Christ has risen from the dead and is alive among us through his Holy Spirit, what of this story would you like Christ to activate in your life?

Emphasis or special occasion: Resurrection Sunday

Chapter 20

The Whole Truth

Luke 24:36-48

Luke was no slouch as a writer. He composed long, convoluted Greek sentences that took half a page to complete. Then, dipping the stylus again into the ink, he suddenly made words on papyrus sound like a 300-year-old, stiff translation of Hebrew into Greek. He subtly repeated themes and patterns of God's grace to help readers hear the Hebrew Old Testament echo in Jesus' life and teaching. The man was a master at clarity: Never a word out of place nor could anyone misunderstand his intent. If one read only Luke's final draft, he'd seem in full command of his subject.

His subject, however, was Jesus, and Jesus had been raised from the dead. No editing job as Luke rewrote Mark's gospel would undo or enhance the earthshaking fact of Jesus' resurrection. Within a few decades the faith had grown out of Judea, and the new religion of Jesus was spreading through the eastern Mediterranean world, even showing up in the city of Rome. This faith was founded upon the truth of Jesus' resurrection.

Luke sat at his writing table. A good writer, yes. A careful historian, of course. A believer in the risen Jesus, always. But in his reporting of Jesus' resurrection appearances, he'd gotten jittery. Luke had his sources. He'd heard the stories passed on from eyewitnesses. Jesus' resurrection was the tip of God's new world invading human existence. As an architect doubts his abilities when asked to design the most imposing structure in the world, so Luke the writer fumbled for words to describe Jesus' three resurrection appearances.

Luke gasped, slammed his hands on the writing table, and stopped his writing halfway through recording Jesus' resurrection appearances. He let his manuscript sit for weeks. Years of work just lay upon a shelf. Daily he walked by the scroll and then quickly left the room. A few fingers' widths of space remained blank on the bottom of the papyrus for the writing of what seemed incredible.

Paul the apostle, decades before, had stumbled around also, trying to describe the resurrection. Paul attempted to do so by talking about different kinds of bodies and the way seeds change after sprouting. Paul struggled to compare what Luke now must portray in order to finish his gospel.

Jesus had been alive and free of the tomb, talking to his students, even eating with them. Luke was sure of this. He interviewed many of the first Christians. They told him about Jesus' simply showing up in their midst. However, if they thought Jesus was a ghost, how could Luke, merely by writing, convince people otherwise? If Jesus' disciples assumed the resurrection was too good to be true, could Luke reduce it to papyrus and seem anything but untrue?

Talk about writer's block! He prayed and checked his notes and written sources again. He discussed the problem with his fellow Christians, and he waited, almost like Jesus told his students to wait in Jerusalem for the power from on high.

Early one Sunday morning it came to him. During a worship gathering, a preacher had talked about Jesus' resurrection. Luke watched Jesus' resurrection appearances in his mind as he heard them. Like in a waking dream he took part in the disciples' experience of Jesus alive again. By an answer to prayer or profound insight, whatever anyone wanted to name it, he realized he needed to tell the story fully. In obedience to God he should record the entire event. Not just that Jesus came out of nowhere while the disciples talked, not just that he commanded them to touch him and reassured them that ghosts weren't made of flesh and blood, not just that he showed them his hands and feet, not just that he ate their broiled fish. In order for readers to truly accept Jesus' final appearance to his disciples, Luke needed to record all the truth. Jesus' resurrection wasn't just about Jesus, but also about the people he appeared to. Luke must tell as much about what Jesus' friends experienced as what Jesus said and did. He dashed into the room where his document about Jesus waited on the shelf.

Luke pulled out the notes about Jesus after his resurrection. He began to copy the events, but he halted in his copying to include what he had been told about Jesus' students. "They were startled and terrified, and thought they were seeing a ghost." He continued reporting Jesus' appearance, but he added that doubts arose in their hearts. He told of how Jesus dealt matter-of-factly with their amazement. Luke then inserted, "in their joy they were disbelieving and still wondering." There it was — the whole truth. He continued the last sentences to describe Jesus' ascension. He pushed the scroll to the side, put his face in his hands, and wept. The whole truth about Jesus' resurrection was now written, and it was almost — but not quite — too good to be true.

Discussion Questions

1. What immediate responses do you have to the story?

2. Do you identify with a character in the story? If yes, how and why do you identify with the person? If no, why don't you identify with anyone in the story?

3. Would you like to have a conversation with a character in the story? What would you say, ask, or suggest to the person? Why?

4. How does the story bring the biblical text into a clearer focus for you?

5. How would you improve or modify the story? Why?

6. How do you picture Jesus' resurrection appearances? Does picturing them help your faith?

7. How do you imagine Jesus' students felt when he appeared to them after his resurrection?

8. If you were to write about Jesus' resurrection appearances, what else would you want to know so you could include it?

9. What further depths of meaning, symbols, connections with, or applications of the biblical faith do you find in the story?

10. Since Jesus Christ has risen from the dead and is alive among us through his Holy Spirit, what of this story would you like Christ to activate in your life?

Emphasis or special occasion: Doubt

Chapter 21

The True Israelite

John 1:43-51; Genesis 28:10-12

The last two months had been difficult for Nathanael and all those around him. The first month he was away from Cana working at Sepphoris; the second month he was back home. At Sepphoris he'd plied his trade plastering cisterns. He'd already spent half his life below ground, working in lamplight, breathing foul air.

When he'd arrived at Sepphoris, Galilee's administrative capital, everyone expected the job to last at least a year, sealing the cisterns being hewn to wind like a labyrinth in the city's bedrock. He worked under both upper and lower Sepphoris, finally leading his crew of nine to the cisterns directly beneath the city's theater.

Nathanael had gained the job because he was the best at plastering cisterns, underground silos, and storage rooms, and only the best could work at Sepphoris, including the city's chief builder, Timaeus of Miletus. Timaeus was, as he said, "In charge of construction from top to bottom." A huge man, he was supported upon thin but flabby legs that had large brown and red splotches. In Aramaic, Nathanael and the crew called him "pig leg" or "pig face," or compared other parts of his body to a pig; yet, they must be careful, because the man seemed to learn their language as fast as he heard it. If he thought they didn't understand his orders in Greek, he was already repeating them in Aramaic.

Timaeus panted down the ladder into the cavern, "Get more over there." It made no difference that they planned to plaster more "over there"; he just yelled. Also, it didn't matter that Nathanael had instructed them where to go next. Timaeus said, "You village Jews! Keep working north. North is that way."

Nathanael tried to do the talking with Timaeus, because Nathanael spoke Greek well. Yet when they spoke, Timaeus seemed to enjoy insulting him: "Take your bunch of village Jews to the southern section," or "Get your stupid village Jews to work."

Nathanael produced only one quality of work: superb. His father had taught him, "Plaster a cistern as though you're the one who'll haul water to it. Prepare it as though you must drink from it. Do the same job for friends, neighbors, or strangers. Not just anyone can be a plasterer. Not just anyone will work honestly for everyone. But you must, because you're a true Israelite artisan."

Three sabbaths passed and Nathanael had endured working for Timaeus. He'd labored for disagreeable people before. But one day, Timaeus came puffing down a ladder into a cavity three times taller than a man. Nathanael was holding himself by one foot on a ladder's rung, the other leg wrapped around the ladder's pole. He grasped a lamp with his left hand and plastered with his right. Timaeus shouted from his ladder to Nathanael, "Hey, you ignorant village Jew, get your men up to the theater fast. They need laborers on the eastern wall."

Nathanael dropped his trowel. "I'm not ignorant," he said as he swung swiftly down the ladder. Timaeus also descended his ladder. Nathanael's crew cringed. If Nathanael were punished for insulting the city's chief builder, they'd suffer, too. Nathanael walked up to Timaeus and held the lamp between them, distorting Timaeus' features. The fat man didn't move. He said, "You sure are. You're an ignorant, illiterate village Jew."

Stepping even closer to Timaeus, Nathanael said through gritted teeth, "I can read," thinking his statement and his expression would silence the Greek. Yet, Timaeus stepped so close to him that his flaccid chest almost touched Nathanael's lamp. "Because you can count Roman mile markers, you think you can read? What language do you read?"

"Hebrew."

"Well, if everyone learned Greek, you wouldn't need another language. Besides, what does reading do for village Jews?" The dim light made Timaeus' sneer look uglier. "What good is it for peasants and rustics to read, above or below ground? Do Jews care about art, beauty, philosophy, or a refined life?"

Nathanael hadn't thought about such things. He made no reply.

"I stand on this hill and admire this beautiful town," Timaeus said, pointing up through the ladder hole. "Sepphoris is the ornament of all Galilee, perched up here like a bird. At the same time, I know that over the hillock to the south you and the other yokels like you in Nazareth won't avail yourself of the enjoyment or the enlightenment of Greek learning."

"I'm not from Nazareth. I'm from the north, Cana."

"No difference," Timaeus said. "You're just like the village Jews in Nazareth — ants working but never changing, destined only to pay taxes to the Romans who'll step on you without a second thought because you're ignorant, village Jews."

"I can read," Nathanael said, raising his voice even higher.

"So what's there to read in your Hebrew language?"

"I read the Torah, God's instruction for holy living."

At this the builder stepped back. If he hadn't, his stomach would have knocked the lamp from Nathanael's hand. He laughed so hard he almost fell, his great bulk tottering upon his tiny, multicolored legs. His laughter echoed through chamber after chamber. "You ignorant village Jew, you ever read anyone else's holy scrolls?"

Nathanael as usual told the truth. "No."

"You read Plato?"

"No."

"You read Aristotle?"

"No."

"You even attend the theater, like the one they're building above your very head, to hear music or behold a tragedy?"

"No," Nathanael said, his voice softer now.

"You foolish village Jews think you're so superior with your one God. Our philosophers figured out there's one God 300 years ago. Did you know that?"

"No," Nathanael said. He'd finished arguing, but Timaeus hadn't.

"I suppose you also scan the horizon daily for your king-messiah to come, and if you don't find him, you scurry up to every teacher with your 'rabbi, rabbi.' But, let's talk about Israel and your holy Torah."

Nathanael's men moved their lamps closer to their work and picked up their pace, granting Nathanael the respect of pretending not to hear.

"You want to brag about Israel. Well, his name was first Jacob, right? Your people are named for Jacob, whose very name meant 'cheat.' He cheated his own brother. And he was a coward and ran away. Of course, that's what your people were always like. I've read the scrolls," he said, pointing to his eyes, "in Greek, of course, and I found that Abraham was a coward and liar. Rebekah helped her son, Jacob, deceive his father and cheat his brother, so that Jacob, whose name finally became 'Israel,' was deceitful all his life. Once Rachel married Jacob, even she stole from her father and lied to him.

"Why would angels ascend and descend upon a ladder — like that one you were working so slowly on — for someone like Jacob, who was fleeing the brother he defrauded? And if angels truly descended for him, why didn't he become better, since you think Jews are so good? How'd you like, as a neighbor, a Jacob who lies, or a Moses who murders, or a David who also commits adultery? Seems they didn't do very well with your *holy* commandments, did they?"

Nathanael finished the day's work, said, "Good-bye," to his crew, and walked to Cana, arriving by midnight. He didn't go back to work. Daily he sat outside the family's house in the shade. His eyes, accustomed to years of working in lamplight, always hurt in the sun. He squinted or simply closed his eyes. He didn't appear to be doing anything, but he was consumed in thought — although he couldn't decide what his effort was recovering from or preparing for. Continually he tossed doubts and questions in his mind and then wondered if a true Israelite would have such doubts.

A month after Nathanael's return, his sister, Shoshanna, came to him, "Nathanael, I brought a baked pigeon."

Nathanael kept his eyes closed. "No, thank you."

"You've got to eat something."

"No, thank you."

"Please, for me."

Nathanael grabbed the dish but closed his eyes again and didn't eat. Shoshanna stood beside him for a while, shuffling her feet occasionally, Nathanael sat motionless, saying nothing.

"You can't let this Greek bother you so much."

Nathanael opened his eyes. "It's not the Greek."

"Then what is it?"

"He's right."

"The Greek? Right about what?"

"About our Torah. I've thought about it. He's right. I didn't know anything about his faith, yet he was right about ours. You and I were taught to be honest and brave. We've been told to do our best and to help our neighbors. But I've searched for good examples in our scriptures, and I don't find many. I don't know what to do."

"Right now, why don't you eat something?"

"No, I don't want to eat." He set the dish down beside him. "I need to figure this out."

"You don't have to understand everything about faith. Faith means not having everything figured out."

"I need *some* things decided, and right now I have none."

"But what about your crew? You can't just leave them."

"If they tell people they've worked for Nathanael of Cana, they can get a job anywhere in lower Galilee." Nathanael picked up the bowl and handed it to Shoshanna then closed his eyes.

"Will you at least come with me to synagogue on the sabbath?"

"No."

That afternoon, Philip arrived from Bethsaida. He'd visited every other week for half a year. Neither he nor Shoshanna were betrothed. Their families were considering their marriage, and Philip and Shoshanna seemed to be helping their families make up their minds.

Philip invited Nathanael to travel with him to the Jordan to hear John the Baptist. At first Nathanael refused, but Philip told of the huge crowds gathering from all of Judea and Jerusalem. Philip said, "Let's find out if John's really a prophet or even the Messiah promised in Moses and the prophets."

"You're chasing a mirage," Nathanael said.

"Well, come on. Let's find out for sure."

"Is there really anything that's sure?"

Philip lifted Nathanael, helped him pack food, and they set out together. On their way, Nathanael told Philip all he could remember that Timaeus said. "It seems Greeks are much more aware of all of life and God than are we Israelites."

"Don't get carried away about how smart the Greeks are."

"Why are you telling me to forget the Greeks? Your grandfather was Greek. You carry a Greek name. You live in a Greek city."

"I trust the almighty God of Israel. Let's go hear John anyway."

The two-day journey exhausted Nathanael. He couldn't decide if by leaving Cana he was seeking or fleeing. He went to the Jordan that afternoon to hear the Baptist preach. The next morning, saying his eyes hurt, Nathanael told Philip that, instead of joining the crowd, he'd pray alone instead.

He was fortunate. He spotted fig trees in the distance, and after a slow, hard climb, he sat down in their shade. He wouldn't be bothered. In Israel, when someone sat under a fig tree, it meant: Join me in pondering God's instruction or leave me to do it alone. Nathanael intended the second. He must solve his problem about Jacob. How could Jacob be the first Israelite when he was so deceitful?

Crowds were gathering to John the Baptist at the Jordan's shore, but that was a long walk away. Here no sound, no rustle of leaves, not even the bleating of goats or sheep grazing near. Sitting among the fig trees was like sitting in a cistern. Nathanael closed his eyes to concentrate. If he talked to Timaeus again, how could he defend Jacob? And the angels ascending and descending near Jacob, what of them? What explanation could Nathanael honestly give, especially for such a deceitful Israelite as Jacob?

Nathanael, eyes closed against the sun, mind tired by questioning, slept and dreamed of angels ascending and descending the ladder in Sepphoris, angels climbing from above ground to beneath, but no one was at the bottom of the ladder. He woke to Philip shaking him. "I've been searching upstream and down for you. We've found him about whom Moses in the law and also the prophets wrote, Jesus son of Joseph from Nazareth."

Nathanael was groggy. He said, "Can anything good come out of Nazareth?"

Philip said to him, "Come and see."

When they neared the Jordan, Jesus spotted them approaching him. He opened his arms wide and said to Nathanael, "Here is truly an Israelite in whom there is no deceit!"

Nathanael was dumbfounded. Through half-closed eyes, he scrutinized this man in front of him, this man whose smile beckoned like a blessing.

"Where did you get to know me?"

"I saw you under the fig tree before Philip called you."

No one had seen where Nathanael sat. Even Philip hadn't known where he was.

"Follow me," Jesus said.

Nathanael felt instantly that Jesus was opposite of Timaeus. Jesus wasn't attacking his doubts, but complimenting his honesty. All Nathanael's feelings and wishes of the last month, all his thoughts and prayers burst from him. "Rabbi, you must be God's Son! You should be Israel's king!"

Jesus answered, "Do you believe because I told you that I saw you under the fig tree? You will see greater things than these. Very truly, I tell you, you will see heaven opened and God's angels ascending and descending upon the Son of Man."

Nathanael endured further trials of faith when Jesus was killed in Jerusalem. After Jesus' resurrection Nathanael was with the disciples at Galilee Lake when Jesus appeared to them and they gained a new understanding of Jesus.

Nathanael didn't return to plastering cisterns and slowly his eyes became used to the sunlight. He trained for a new job and did it well: teaching that Jesus honored people who had honest doubts and questions. His new, happy labor was to receive others as Jesus had received him. He explained that despite the imperfections of their Jewish forebears, all the dreams of their scriptures came true in Jesus whom Nathanael, the true Israelite, worshiped as God's Son, Israel's king.

Discussion Questions

1. What immediate responses do you have to the story?

2. Do you identify with a character in the story? If yes, how and why do you identify with the person? If no, why don't you identify with anyone in the story?

3. Would you like to have a conversation with a character in the story? What would you say, ask, or suggest to the person? Why?

4. How does the story bring the biblical text into a clearer focus for you?

5. How would you improve or modify the story? Why?

6. Have you met a non-Christian who knew more about Christianity than you did about his or her religion?

7. What's it like to believe in Jesus (which means to believe in a particular religion) when so many people believe that all religions are the same?

8. Has someone helped you with your doubts? What doubts have you learned to live with?

9. What further depths of meaning, symbols, connections with, or applications of the biblical faith do you find in the story?

10. Since Jesus Christ has risen from the dead and is alive among us through his Holy Spirit, what of this story would you like Christ to activate in your life?

Chapter 22

Upside Down

John 2:13-22

Dear Reverend Doctor Fitz,

I have never written to a bishop before, but necessity compels me. Circumstances at the Saint Andrew Church have reached an impasse. A number of longtime members are no longer worshiping here and the new people who have come are not supporting the church's activities, as did those faithful who have gone before us. Upon careful thought and persistent discussion with the pillars of this church, I have decided to write to you in order to state my grave concerns about, and profound disagreements with, our pastor, Richard Dodd.

He has been employed here for more than a year; therefore, we have endured him through four seasons. It became apparent soon after his arrival that he would be nothing but problems. In less than a month, he ruined his welcome. My husband has been treasurer of this congregation for more than 24 years. Pastor Dodd asked him why he listed in the bulletin the contributions that people made to pay for the radio broadcast each Sunday.

"People like to see their names there," my husband said.

"We don't list money that other members give for special needs, nor do we report what people contribute week by week to the general budget," he said. "Why would we publicly announce what a few people give for a particular ministry?"

"Reverend Dodd, my wife and I are honoring our fathers and mothers by giving this as a memorial," my husband said, very properly. "No one ever suggested printing regular giving in the bulletin."

"Mr. Murphy," Pastor Dodd said, "the Bible gives a lot of leeway on many things. But on a few, we have straightforward guidance. Jesus said that we shouldn't let our left hand know what our right hand is doing. He's talking about our giving anonymously."

My husband, perfectly sizing up the situation said, "*My* left hand knows well what *my* right hand is doing, and no one has ever complained about doing it this way."

The gall! Also, on our annual Children's Sunday, he wore a Hawaiian shirt to worship and served communion to the children that way, saying that sometimes we need to be bright and happy at the Lord's altar instead of sad and mopey. You're the theologian. I'm sure you can judge that one.

He insists we sing some little ditties (he calls them choruses) in worship before we can raise our reverent voices in the grand hymns of the faith. When people very calmly and correctly expressed their dissatisfaction with such songs, he said that as Jesus told individuals they had to lose their life for his sake, churches also have to die to the things they like in order to do ministry for people who are different than they are. He said that's Jesus' pattern. We think that's *his* pattern for *this* church.

It gets worse. He has been a smart aleck almost to the point of being blasphemous. He spoke hideously about our ladies' aide bazaar. Our ladies aide has always held a bazaar the week before Easter to pay for various necessities in the church, such as kitchen supplies. Also, every year we choose one room or part of the church for remodeling and decorating. Our bazaar has been quite successful. We call it the "holy emporium." We offer the townspeople a chance to get real bargains on beautiful crafts. Our church is much the more attractive for all the dedicated work the ladies (and their husbands) have put in over the years.

I suppose it was because of what Pastor Dodd had said to my husband that led me (in the presence of three other ladies, mind you) to ask him what he thought of our holding a bazaar in the church. I mean, who knows what crazy schemes roll around in his head, especially since he took such unexplainable actions as deleting the "Gloria Patri" and "Doxology" from the worship bulletin and replacing them with "Glory Be To The Father" and "Praise God." He tells us we're supposed to figure out why.

Well, at the question of the church having a bazaar, the young man smiled and said, "I have nothing against having a bazaar in the church building." We ladies sighed in relief as we turned to go. "But," he said, and we turned to listen, "if a bearded man — about thirty years old — in a robe and sandals comes in and starts turning over tables, I wouldn't advise trying to stop him."

The nerve. If I were to summarize his impact upon this church, it would be to say that he's turned *everything* upside down. I hope and expect that you will be swift and sure in dealing with this problem, because if not, from all the evidence, this church is soon going to die.

Very sincerely yours,
Mrs. Emma O'Connor Murphy

Discussion Questions

1. What immediate responses do you have to the story?

2. Do you identify with a character in the story? If yes, how and why do you identify with the person? If no, why don't you identify with anyone in the story?

3. Would you like to have a conversation with a character in the story? What would you say, ask, or suggest to the person? Why?

4. How does the story bring the biblical text into a clearer focus for you?

5. How would you improve or modify the story? Why?

6. Where and when have you seen church traditions challenged?

7. Which church traditions most need to be maintained? Why? Which church traditions most need to be jettisoned? Why?

8. How do you decide between the necessity of maintaining our Christian heritage and the necessity of employing different ministry methods in each new age?

9. What further depths of meaning, symbols, connections with, or applications of the biblical faith do you find in the story?

10. Since Jesus Christ has risen from the dead and is alive among us through his Holy Spirit, what of this story would you like Christ to activate in your life?

Emphasis or special occasion: Christmas

Chapter 23

Fifty Feet Below Molly's Face

John 3:6-8; Isaiah 9:6

The trail was either dust or mud with little transition between the two. Rick was ahead, gasping as much as I. His pack was heavier, since he carried the raft. We were warm, but at least not burning hot, as we'd been a few times on this trail. Rick puffed out his cheeks as we stopped to wheeze, get the wobble out of our legs, and slow our breathing. "Turning fifty has no redeeming social value," he said, rivulets of sweat running down his cheeks.

We shifted our packs and panted a while, thumbs under our shoulder straps. I looked down the grade we'd climbed. "It didn't seem as steep thirty years ago. You sure you want to keep going?"

Rick turned and started up the trail. I knew he would. Although we'd lived 200 miles apart for 31 years, only three times had we missed meeting for our yearly two days of hiking and fishing. Rick and I were the same age. I was from Wilhelm. He grew up in our rival: McPherson. All through high school, although we didn't know one another, we competed. McPherson beat us three of four years in football, but senior year we ruined their homecoming, scoring the winning touchdown in the last 51 seconds. Our basketball games were usually won by the home team. Senior year in track I flew a foot higher than he did in the pole vault, but he destroyed me in the high hurdles.

The summer after our freshman year in college we finally met, working at Compton's Lumber Mill. McPherson was eight miles north of the mill and Wilhelm thirteen miles southeast. After a couple weeks stacking lumber with half a dozen guys, I realized I had more in common with Rick Hoisington than with anyone else. We became partners in the mill and friends beyond it. He was my atheist friend. I didn't bludgeon him with Bible verses, but I told him of my faith. A few times he said, "I know others believe, but I don't. I search my heart and I don't know why, but I don't believe — like some people don't have freckles and don't know why they don't have freckles."

During the first summer we worked together Compton's Mill held a picnic. The flyer taped to the time clock announced free food and sodas and included swing shift's challenging day shift to a softball game. It was obvious why. Swing shift had a lot of good ball players — permanents and summer help alike. The permanents on days were mostly older, a lot of them busted up from logging accidents. Rick and I took a quick count of those from day shift healthy enough or foolish enough to risk life and limb on the softball field. Including us, the number was nine.

I asked, "You any good at softball?"

"Are you kidding? Why do you suppose I ran track?"

"I wouldn't mind playing," I said, "if I'd only be in a couple innings. But I'd need a radar assist to hit a ball. What do you want to do?"

Rick tucked the last two-by-six into a stack of sixteen footers and began banding the package. "Well, we could go fishing and tell everybody we'd planned it before the picnic was announced."

That was our story and we stuck to it. We made it partially true by going fishing. We drove an hour and a half to a trailhead of the Pacific Crest Trail. Rick drove his dad's old Dodge Dart slowly so it wouldn't heat up, leaving plenty of time to talk. We'd only been stacking lumber together for a month and, although we'd told most of our jokes, compared our freshman year at college, replayed every athletic contest we'd ever participated in, and named all our buddies and their idiosyncrasies, we'd never identified girls we both knew. Other than my cousin, Diane, who attended McPherson in the second grade, I didn't know any girls from his school.

"You know any from Wilhelm?"

"Just one who I was interested in, Molly. Met her at a dance, junior year," Rick said as we both leaned forward to read the sign to the trailhead. "I'm not sure about her last name."

"Molly Vester?"

"Yeah, that's her. You know Molly?"

"Know her? She was my neighbor through most of school. She's going to MIT."

Rick turned onto the narrow gravel road and the trees closed in around us. "MIT? Speaks well for her mind. I might have been intrigued by her mind. But she talked so slowly that after a few dances and time out for refreshments, I lost interest in her mind *and* her body."

"That's Molly — born in Mississippi, moved to Oregon in fourth grade."

"She was really pretty," Rick said.

"In high school she started working on her hair and using more makeup."

"That's the usual age."

"Objectively, I could say she was gorgeous, but we knew one another so long, she was almost like my sister. Plus, in sixth grade she broke my bicycle and wouldn't admit it even when our parents were gone and I said I wasn't mad anymore."

That first hike into Mystic Lake was thrilling, partly because of the excitement of lying to the guys at the mill and forcing them to cancel the softball game, and partly because Rick and I didn't have a real map and I'd forgotten my compass, and with side trails entering every few miles, we had difficulty following Harry's instructions. Harry cooked at the Alpine restaurant across from the mill, and on a paper napkin, he'd sketched a wiggly line he said was roughly the trail. All we really knew was that about ten miles north of the trailhead a lake appeared on the right and a high cliff on the left, below which were three forest service lean-tos. After over four hours of hard climbing and holding a conference over the napkin at each trail crossing, we arrived. I looked at the lake, Rick looked at the cliff.

"I'm going to kill some fish," I said.

Rick grabbed my arm and pointed up. "She's still with us."

"Huh?"

"Molly."

"Molly Vester?" I asked.

"Look."

Halfway up the cliff, an eight foot-rock protruded. "Molly's nose," I said.

"They couldn't have done better on Mount Rushmore."

We laughed ourselves silly over that nose, and no matter what some forest service map might have named the camp, to us it was always just below Molly's Face, and we greeted her every year, "Hello, Molly, old girl."

This year, after almost six hours of hiking, when we finally saw Molly's Face, Rick said, "Hello, Molly old, *old* girl."

He dropped his pack with a groan as I did mine and I said, "She's definitely aging."

We didn't make camp. A wind was coming up and we wanted to fish before nightfall. I rigged the rods while Rick pumped up the little raft. We'd never tried a raft before, but brush had grown on shore, leaving few places to fish from the bank. Rick commented that the shoreline needed a good fire to clean it out.

"Or some selective logging," I said.

"Could you see these six-foot diameters going through Compton's Mill? Used to be logs that size, now they just cut big toothpicks."

By the time we were fishing, the wind was blowing harder from the southwest, but we were at the lake's northeast corner. If we had problems, we'd let the wind blow us to shore. We took turns rowing. The raft was almost too light to maneuver — even the oars were plastic — and it was small. We were crushed together. By the second time our lines tangled, the wind changed, and we were being blown a little to the south. But we were able to row into the wind and make enough headway for action on our lures. We were getting lots of bites, which was exciting, because each time one of us jerked his rod to set the hook, he kicked the other guy.

While I was landing my second fish — Rick had three — we felt the raft pushed to the side by a gust from the west.

"Holy smoke," Rick said. "We're in for it."

The wind had changed 120 degrees since we put in and was blowing us away from camp and toward the middle of the lake. If the wind blew us to the south bank, it would be a five-mile hike back.

"Let's head for camp," I said. But I didn't need to. Rick was at the oars and he was turning as I reeled in our lines. Then a second blast caught us broadside and nearly dunked us. The wind seemed to explode from nowhere. Each wave lifted and dropped us with a thud. Rick shouted over the wind, "If it doesn't get any worse, we can make it."

It got worse. A cloud bank, not a cloud, but an advancing wing of clouds, swept over the lake, instantly covering Molly's Face, and the rain advanced like a wall. When it hit us, we were already soaking wet, yet the rain was frigid.

After fifteen minutes, Rick said, "I'm exhausted. I'll turn and you row."

This wasn't easy, even though we merely spun the raft around. We nearly tipped over. I rowed for all that the flimsy oars and I were worth. I probably kept going for ten minutes and was panting so hard I could barely swallow. We were still a quarter mile from shore and even over the sound of the rain we could hear the wind roaring through the trees. After another tricky pivot, Rick rowed. With my aching hands, I held onto the rope around the raft, gasped back my breath and pointed if he got off course.

Twice more we swiveled the raft and changed the rower. Finally, we edged a bit into the lee of Molly's Face. The rain was lessening. Our hands were numb, our arms and backs throbbed. Whether rowing or hanging on we shook with cold and exhaustion in a raft sloshing full of water.

Rick was at the oars when finally each stroke granted significant movement. He spun the raft so he could push instead of pull, and I got ready to leap onto the shore and yank us up. I jumped too soon and was in up to my waist. Yet, I held the rope. On shore, we lay in the mud for ten minutes, gasping, spitting, puffing, and grunting. It was a while before I was able to speak. "I think I was praying as hard as I was rowing," I said.

"Me, too," Rick said.

Even though I'm hard of hearing from all the summers in the mill, I knew I heard him correctly. We were cold and tired and needed to get a fire started and camp prepared before dark. I managed to get up first. "When I went into the drink, I banged into our string of fish. They're still there."

"That's supper," Rick said.

It was a pretty good supper, along with granola bars and tea. We huddled in the lean-to with a fire just outside. The wind from behind Molly's Face decreased, the sky cleared, and an hour or so of huddling near the fire warmed us. Even if we were still damp, we were grateful for being together beneath Molly's Face. Our escape from danger made us as giddy as middle school girls. We chattered about Wild Bill the sawyer, assuming he was still in jail; and Johnny Decker, who was killed in Vietnam; and Charlie Murray, who hurried home every lunch to make sure his wife hadn't left him, and Bernie Delay, whom everybody called "Be Delayed."

We shifted around the fire until late. We finally crawled into our sleeping bags and slowed our talking a bit. We lay quietly until I said, "When we got to shore I said I'd been praying. You said you had, too."

"Uh-huh."

"You didn't used to pray. You didn't believe in God."

"I do now."

I lay there in the dark waiting for him to say more. "Well...?"

"Cheryl," he said.

I'd met Cheryl when they were engaged. It was hard to say whether Cheryl was Rick's second, third, or fourth wife. He lived with a girl for a year in college, then a couple years out of college married Joyce. They had four children as quickly as humans could conceive and give birth and within a decade they divorced. A few years later he lived with Donna, but only a few months.

"Before I met her, I'd begun to wonder what was wrong with the women in this world. But I wanted to marry Cheryl and decided she'd be my last wife. She assured me she'd have it no other way, and she wouldn't marry anyone who didn't attend church. I said, 'But I don't believe in God.'

" 'I don't care,' she said. 'You don't have to believe in God to go to church; but I won't be going to church without my husband. You attend worship with me or I won't marry you.'

" 'I don't have anything against church,' I said. 'It just seems hypocritical of me to go.'

" 'Rick, I went to the Blazers game with you,' she said, 'and watched them play the Slakers.'

" 'You're not funny,' I said.

" 'Before I went to the game, I didn't believe in basketball. While I was there, I didn't believe in basketball. I still don't believe in basketball. Yet if you ask me, I'll go, because you want me to and because I love you.'

"We were married, and every Sunday we went to church. I never had anything against church, I just didn't believe."

"I know," I said.

"So, we'd been worshiping for a few months and I liked the people. I haven't gotten used to the robes and candles and stuff, but the pastor is okay. Cheryl was so proud to have me with her. It was last Christmas. The choir and the congregation sang back and forth. It was kind of fun, like tennis. It went on a little too long, but the words and melody were haunting, 'Wonderful Counselor, Mighty God, Everlasting Father, Prince of Peace.' Sort of hypnotic. The next Sunday, holding hands, Cheryl and I walked into the church and down the aisle to the fifth pew from the front on the left — her spot — and all down the aisle the song from the week before was singing in my mind. Just as I sat, I realized I believed it. One minute I didn't believe. For no reason the next moment I did, and I couldn't explain why.

"I blinked out for a few minutes, didn't say, 'Hello,' to people around me or join the call to worship and that stuff. I just sat there and searched my heart. I believed, and I would always believe. Before I listened for God, sometimes even wanted to believe. It was as though I looked at the sky, like right now, yet saw only the darkness. Now I see the stars. I'm getting used to believing. I've been wanting to tell you."

It was hard for me to respond. All I could say was, "I'm honored you'd tell me. I'm happy for you."

I reached across for him in the dark and we shook hands. We didn't say much more. It was around midnight. Each of us was tired from driving to the trailhead and then thoroughly exhausted from the hike and our little spin on the lake.

We woke with the dawn, caught our limit in an hour or so, caught and released another dozen, packed, and hiked down to the trailhead.

We shook hands at our cars and I said, "Good-bye, friend."

"And more than a friend," Rick said.

I look forward to next year's two days of hiking and fishing more than to all the year's holidays rolled up together.

* * *

A Possible Addition To The Story

Jesus says, "What is born of the flesh is flesh, and what is born of the Spirit is spirit. Do not be astonished that I said to you, 'You must be born from above.' The wind blows where it chooses, and you hear the sound of it, but you do not know where it comes from or where it goes. So it is with everyone who is born of the Spirit."

Think about how God's Spirit, over the years, has breathed upon you and blown you upon a new life course....

Consider how God's Spirit, across the miles, has swirled you around and aimed you toward abundant life....

Let us pray: Our loving God in heaven, thank you for your faithfulness to us. Thank you that you have sought us wherever we have gone. We praise you that our sin does not stop your love and that our unbelief does not halt your pursuit of us. With relief and joy we surrender our lives to your love, and accept all the blessings and tasks that you have so long wanted to grant us.

In the name of your Son, Jesus, we pray. Amen.

Discussion Questions

1. What immediate responses do you have to the story?

2. Do you identify with a character in the story? If yes, how and why do you identify with the person? If no, why don't you identify with anyone in the story?

3. Would you like to have a conversation with a character in the story? What would you say, ask, or suggest to the person? Why?

4. How does the story bring the biblical text into a clearer focus for you?

5. How would you improve or modify the story? Why?

6. Have you had a friend or spouse who helped your faith, or whose faith you helped?

7. Have you learned how to share your faith without threatening or demeaning others?

8. Have you had a similar experience to what Rick had, being especially touched by a scripture or a song in worship? What was the scripture or song and what was the outcome in your life?

9. What further depths of meaning, symbols, connections with, or applications of the biblical faith do you find in the story?

10. Since Jesus Christ has risen from the dead and is alive among us through his Holy Spirit, what of this story would you like Christ to activate in your life?

Emphasis or special occasion: The Lord's Supper

Chapter 24

And What Else?

John 6:1-21

"The wind was squealing through the rigging," Peter said. "We'd gotten the sail down and were doing our best to row into the wind. It was tougher than we'd faced for a long time — especially at night. Half of us rowed, half bailed. We all prayed."

Peter shifted his weight. His old bones hurt after sitting long in any position. He reclined with his students on the evening before they would leave on their preaching missions. Peter trained them as Jesus trained him. At this farewell meal he continued, "We weren't thinking much about Jesus right then, but he's the one who got us there. He healed lots of people. They glommed onto him, like they were trying to filch power from him. To get time alone we sailed to the east shore, but a large crowd kept following us. They'd seen how many people he healed.

"Boat after boat scraped onto the shore and people leaped out and splashed up to us. We looked north and saw crowds walking from there. They were all converging on Jesus. He led us up the hill and had us sit. He surveyed the crowd and said to Philip, 'Where are we to buy bread for these people to eat?' "

Peter paused, leaned to the side, and said, "The Romans don't have cushions as good as we had in Galilee." His students laughed. He stretched his back and said to his students, "I've told you, haven't I, about the people on the hillside?" His students nodded.

"Well, Jesus knew what he was going to do, but we didn't understand it at the time. Philip answered him, 'Six months' wages couldn't buy enough bread for each of them to get a little.'

"My brother, Andrew, said to him, 'A boy's here with five barley loaves and two fish. But what's that for so many people?' By that time about 5,000 people were on the hillside. Jesus gave thanks for the loaves and distributed them and the fish — as much as everybody wanted. Then he had us gather the leftovers and they filled twelve baskets. Everybody had eaten in their own group, and it wasn't until they looked around and saw how much was left over that they realized what happened. This was another miracle. Jesus fed the multitude. Surely he was the prophet. They wanted to toss Jesus onto their shoulders and take him to Jerusalem as king. But he realized what they were doing and retreated alone up the hill.

"When it was evening and he didn't return, we got in our boat, as everyone else had done, and started back to Capernaum. When Jesus wanted to be alone, we'd learned to leave him alone. However, we hadn't learned enough from the miracles he'd done, not even the one he performed that day, the miracle whose fragments we collected in twelve baskets.

"Have I told you this before?" the old man asked.

"Yes, but go on," his disciples said, "Tell us about Jesus walking on the lake."

"All right, but you must be ready to finish this story for me," Peter said. "That's when we were fighting for headway, smack in the middle of the lake. Believe me, the importance of the day's events was lost on us in the dark. We could hardly see one another. We kept yelling over the wind so that the rowers stroked together. We who were bailing encouraged the rowers, because no matter how tired they were of rowing, we couldn't stop and switch rowers. We were," he held two fingers close together, "that near to going under. We barely controlled the boat, not half a bowl of strength left among us. We talked about it afterward. We'd all lost hope, and at that moment none of us thought of Jesus and his power.

"That's when we saw Jesus walking on the sea and coming near the boat. If we thought we were frightened by the storm, we were terrified when we saw him. But he said, 'It is I; do not be afraid.' We wanted to get him into our boat, but at that moment we reached the shore at Capernaum.

"Now," the aged Peter moved slightly from his reclining position at the table. He rotated his arm to get the feeling back, "now, you finish the story."

"You just did," the youngest student said.

"No," Peter instructed him. "I told you what happened. It's not enough to remember what Jesus did, as it's insufficient merely to repeat the words of his teaching. We must understand what Jesus' words and deeds mean today. When you leave tomorrow on your missions, you'll encounter people who need more than a report about what Jesus did decades ago. Now, you finish my story."

The group was silent for some time as Peter looked at them, one by one, face by face. Finally, a young man next to Peter said haltingly, "Jesus is with us in the storm."

"True," Peter said, "go on."

From the back, an older man caught on and said, "Jesus will come to us when we don't expect him."

"At the very least, yes," Peter said, "and what else?"

Someone said quickly, "His multiplying the bread and fish is also what he does today when we remember him in this meal."

Peter nodded, "Go on."

After a pause, a student in the middle of the group said, "Jesus arrives even when we aren't thinking about him."

"Certainly," Peter said, "and what else?"

Discussion Questions

1. What immediate responses do you have to the story?

2. Do you identify with a character in the story? If yes, how and why do you identify with the person? If no, why don't you identify with anyone in the story?

3. Would you like to have a conversation with a character in the story? What would you say, ask, or suggest to the person? Why?

4. How does the story bring the biblical text into a clearer focus for you?

5. How would you improve or modify the story? Why?

6. Has a Christian teacher pushed you to a further, necessary understanding of Jesus? How?

7. What's an insight into Jesus' miracles that you have only gained after years of being a Christian?

8. What would you say that this text also leads us to believe and to expect from Jesus?

9. What further depths of meaning, symbols, connections with, or applications of the biblical faith do you find in the story?

10. Since Jesus Christ has risen from the dead and is alive among us through his Holy Spirit, what of this story would you like Christ to activate in your life?

Emphasis or special occasion: Resurrection Sunday

Chapter 25

Lazarus: Second Death, Third Life

John 11:1-13, 38-44

In ancient Palestine, most children died before their mid-teens. Perhaps only 3% of people lived to be sixty. Thus, to be elderly was to be out of the ordinary and obviously blessed. Older people were honored and deferred to and sought out for advice and spiritual guidance. An aged person must be wise, and much older meant much wiser, and one about to die of great age was viewed as richest in knowledge and regarded with awe.

This morning we gather with the relatives and friends of Jesus' aged friend, Lazarus. Decades ago, Jesus raised Lazarus from the dead, summoned him from the tomb, gave him life, and gave him back to his sisters and to his community. This morning, Lazarus is dying for the second time and we are invited to his house. We draw near to him not only to pay our respects and to offer our prayers, but to receive the blessing of one so obviously blessed.

Lazarus lies on a simple bed. He turns to us as we arrive. "I'm glad you've come, friends," he says with difficulty. "You didn't have to. I tried to make that clear in the message. I just wanted to see you before I leave you for a second time. I'm old and dying; but, despite a bachelor's joy in his nieces and nephews, I haven't summoned you simply so I could glory in family and friends. Now that my days are few, I want to speak once more about living and dying. I know about these. Oh, younger people know so much nowadays. You know of Jesus' teachings and what was said against him. You know the Romans killed him and we say that wasn't the end of him.

"It has been more than forty years now since the master walked among us. Since then the world has changed. Our holy city is destroyed. In Jerusalem's streets lie the stones that were once our temple, and we're servants of a Rome that has also changed. We now have Christian brothers and sisters in Rome, and more than once they've sent money to sustain us through famine. They also send news of how the world is changing because of the message of our Lord's resurrection.

"What? No, I'm sorry, I didn't hear you. Resurrection? You don't like that word, do you, my young friend? Why must I say, 'Resurrection'? Yes, it's important. I don't blame you for asking. Even the rabbis, who still resist Jesus' message, believe in a future resurrection.

"But to tell of Jesus' resurrection I must tell of me. I expect you've heard of my younger life. Chances are, everything you heard is true. When I was young, I was a skeptic. I listened to the philosophers and I was pretty sure that religion was magic and superstition. It was good for frightened children, guilty old men, and ugly girls. But religion held nothing for me. I lived as I wished. May the Lord bless Mary and Martha. They kept me in their home no matter what disgraceful things I said or did. Our parents were dead. Our uncles were dead, and we lived alone. Mary and Martha worked hard to keep a comfortable home. I worked a little. I was the neighborhood outrage. I did nothing very wrong. I was mostly lazy and obstinate. Mary and Martha couldn't change me. They loved me and prayed for me.

"I remember the spring when Mary and Martha went to Jerusalem. I was sick. Since Jerusalem was just over the hill, they stayed with me before joining the last of the pilgrims. They came home late with Jesus and his followers. I felt better the moment Jesus walked in the door. I liked him first thing. I was intrigued with his speaking of God as our Father. I hadn't had a father for a long time.

"That night I, too, became his follower. Don't get me wrong. I wasn't a believer. But after hearing him and seeing his concern for the ill and suffering, other teachers were nothing. The others? It was as if a city were under attack, and while the citizens flocked to the walls in its defense, the priests were in the marketplace pricing material for new worship gowns. The Pharisees were like picnickers sitting on a hill watching the battle; instead of caring for the people, they loudly lamented the world's evil.

"After I heard Jesus, the Sadducees with their insistence on just the law and their shunning the prophets are like men watching a sculptor and, being pleased with his first strokes, beg him to carve no more from his rock because it is sufficient, although hardly begun.

"And the scribes. It was as if a man came to the village and told a story filled with all the truth about God and humanity. All who heard it went away determined to love one another and obey God — except the scribes who sat together and wrote funny poems about the storyteller. The angels laugh at those men. Compared to Jesus, the other teachers were mapmakers who drew maps without ever seeing the territory.

"Jesus not only spoke to us and listened to our problems, he helped us, cared for us — more than for himself. Then it seemed we couldn't be more oppressed. Merchants swindled us in the temple. Soldiers spat on us in the streets. Tax collectors pillaged our very homes with their extortion.

"Jesus was gentle in meeting human need. Other rabbis didn't allow women to follow them. Jesus' love captured Mary and Martha. Mary anointed his feet with perfume and wiped them with her hair. You know respectable Jewish women don't appear in public with hair unbound. I was his friend, too. He was really the only man I loved. Jesus accepted our love. He came to our home often, sometimes alone, sometimes with Peter or the others. Peter and I became friends and we often speculated about the Messiah's coming.

"Jesus was so much like the rest of us, yet always different. He played with children, ate and drank, and was gloriously happy. Then he talked all night, telling us what God was like, explaining how God treated everyone equally because God cared for us all the same. Jesus walked miles, preaching, teaching, and healing people. Yet in his weariness he was alert and kind to those near him. It's not true when people say Jesus wasn't human because he was never tired. They didn't know him. He was, perhaps, the most tired man ever. He was burdened by people, exhausted by our needs. Crowds flocked to him, asking for his hand to bless, his smile to ease pain, and his word to heal. So many took strength from him, only a few offered strength in return. We all failed him.

"Then I became sick again. I'd never been physically strong. I didn't know what it was this time, but I feared I'd die.

"No. No. Let the child cry. I don't mind. I don't blame him for the fuss. Let him cry. His cry is honest. His cry says he's hungry or uncomfortable. He's better off than we who yearn for a word from God but are too proud to ask. I think that's why Jesus loved children so much.

"Where was I? Yes, as I was saying, I died. I died half in belief and hope, half in disbelief and despair. We'd sent for Jesus. He didn't come.

"Has someone wakened you from a dream, and, as they spoke your name, you didn't know whether you were hearing someone in the dream or hearing someone waking you? That's what it was like to be born again. I can't describe the sensation of breathing again and moving my arms and legs. When I stepped from the tomb, someone took the cloth from my face. The sunlight burned my eyes and I squinted, but the warmth was so good. The air smelled so fresh. Everyone began to yell. Mary and Martha cried. Then we all laughed and shouted and praised God. Jesus was hitting me on the back and laughing and I didn't ask him why he tarried in coming.

"Soon he left and I became a notable person. Officials came from Jerusalem to determine if I'd really died. Pharisees interrogated me. Everyone wanted to know what it was like to die and wake again and I struggled to put it into words. But lots of people didn't believe I'd really died, and I became angry with them. I'd changed little. Though I now believed Jesus, I hadn't the slightest thought of changing my life. But did I have a time of it! Everyone invited me to feasts of the best food and wine. Mary and Martha were too happy I was alive to scold me for pride in my life's new position.

"That was late winter. A few weeks later, Jesus returned to Jerusalem for purification and rode into Jerusalem like a hero. People waved palm fronds and shouted praises to God. I was a hero, too. People pointed me out and parents brought their children for me to bless. A rumor went around that the chief priests were out to kill Jesus and me. That made me more of a celebrity. A crowd followed me all day. I was giddy with their attention.

"Less than a week later, on the evening of Passover, some friends threw a party in my honor in Bethany. Since Jerusalem's hyper-orthodox snobs could disagree about how to celebrate Passover, and since the Essenes could disagree with them all, we kept Passover our irreverent way. We partook of Passover's four cups of wine with our families. Then after the meal we left our families to have more wine. We drank almost until morning.

"I was dead asleep when Peter tumbled into the house, crying, blubbering, and talking incoherently. 'They've got him. I lied. Going to kill him,' he said. My head was thick and he could tell I didn't understand. He grabbed me and shook me violently. 'They're going to kill Jesus. They've taken him to Golgotha. I ran away.' He screamed a loud, mournful shriek and slapped me, out of contempt for himself I think, and ran out into the morning.

"By the afternoon, when I finally got up courage to go to Jerusalem, Jesus was dead. His mother was standing beside his cross with a few women. They turned to me, and by their sorrowful looks I was convicted and sentenced. My absence at Jesus' dying was a curse upon me. I glanced once more at the man I'd said I loved, then I left.

"For two days, I wandered alone. I'd spent time in the grave before, but this was worse. I walked the road from Bethany to Jerusalem. When I got to Jerusalem I couldn't bear the memory of the women at Jesus' cross. But as I neared Bethany I couldn't halt there, having disappointed my sisters. I spent two days as a lost man on the road between Jerusalem and Bethany.

"On the first day of the week, Peter came running and yelling from behind me. He grasped me, laughing, gasping, and hiccupping. 'He's alive,' he yelled. Tears running down his face. 'He's alive. I've seen him,' he shouted at the top of his voice. 'The Lord lives. He's been resurrected.'

"At that moment, though I didn't know why — then or now — I believed him. My spirit knew, although my mind didn't understand. Jesus was alive, as alive as I was. And I? I was finally alive, completely alive, eternally alive. Since then I've constantly borne witness to Jesus' resurrection.

"But I'm rambling. Yes, I'm rambling. Perhaps older people are more concerned with truth than with the vessel truth is carried in. But what isn't rambling is that Jesus the Messiah was the vessel in which all of God's truth was carried. By my life's miracle I promise you, Jesus carried God's truth in love every day until his last.

"I don't have much strength left, but I need to tell you this: You've heard that the Lord delayed in coming when I was sick. He said, 'Our friend Lazarus has fallen asleep.' Now I understand, and I don't fear my second death. For Christians, death is real, very real, but it's only as real as sleep. I've died once and felt Jesus' love bring me back to life. I anticipate a third life. As people lie down to sleep expecting to wake in the morning, I lie down to die expecting most certainly to wake and to see my friend Jesus — laughing.

"Gather closer. Come ... yes, closer. As I've so richly received it, I now grant you the eternal blessing of our risen Lord Jesus Christ."

Discussion Questions

1. What immediate responses do you have to the story?

2. Do you identify with a character in the story? If yes, how and why do you identify with the person? If no, why don't you identify with anyone in the story?

3. Would you like to have a conversation with a character in the story? What would you say, ask, or suggest to the person? Why?

4. How does the story bring the biblical text into a clearer focus for you?

5. How would you improve or modify the story? Why?

6. What do you imagine it was like for Lazarus to be brought back from the dead?

7. Have you experienced your own way of dying and being brought back to life by Jesus? Have you been miraculously healed or spared? How did it change you?

8. Do you think much about death and eternal life? When do you think about it least? Most?

9. What further depths of meaning, symbols, connections with, or applications of the biblical faith do you find in the story?

10. Since Jesus Christ has risen from the dead and is alive among us through his Holy Spirit, what of this story would you like Christ to activate in your life?

Chapter 26

John's Final Revision

John 21:20-25; John 14:18; John 16:13

Tradition holds that Jesus' disciple, John, survived to a great age. He died in Ephesus in the Roman province of Asia on the coast of today's Turkey. While exiled to the nearby island of Patmos, John beheld the visions now recorded in the Bible's book of Revelation, and over the years he sent three letters important enough to be saved and included in our New Testament. Last, after a lifetime of preaching, teaching, and explaining the meaning of Jesus' words and deeds, he compiled a narrative of Jesus' ministry now bearing the name "The Gospel according to John."

Jesus had promised, "When the Spirit of truth comes, he will guide you into all the truth." Trusting what Jesus said and aware of Jesus' Holy Spirit within him, John found it hard to stop writing about Jesus. Every time he thought he was finished, he remembered something to include of what Jesus said or did — even though some of his additions didn't fit well with what he already wrote.

John was very old and immediately after he judged his chronicle of good news finally complete, he recognized the need to append another incident. Lately, more than once his students asked, "What will happen to us if you die?" When they questioned him, "Will Jesus return before you die?" John decided to add to his gospel record the event of Jesus' last meeting with his students.

John set aside this second day of the week to approach his writing table for a final time. He'd write what so obviously needed to be attached to his gospel. He vowed, "Lord Jesus, if you allow me these few words ... If you grant this one last memory of you onto papyrus ... If you so will, let me add this concluding episode and I promise, then, to circulate this account of your good news to all corners of the world."

Slowly, more slowly than usual, John now ascended the grand street of Ephesus, pondering what and how to write. His knees seemed to scream in pain with every step. He planned an earlier start for today's labor of writing, but this morning three of his students were arguing angrily with a Judean. John stepped into the quarrel to silence them. He sent away the Judean with an apology and a blessing. John, who was one of the hotheads among Jesus' students, now said to his own students, "You can't win converts by arguing."

"Our Lord Jesus argued," Crates said. "You told us he did — many times."

"Correct." John smiled at the earnest young man. "But our Lord Jesus argued with people and loved them at the same time."

John forgot the day's planned writing (and his bodily pains) as he spent the morning reviewing with his students how Jesus disagreed with people in ways that allowed them insight into themselves and God. Only after the midday meal did John again start toward Rhianus' home. After Rhianus became a Christian, he presented to John a room on the second floor of his house with an outside staircase. There, John enjoyed the silence needed for prayer or to prepare to teach. There, also, John wrote his letters and, slowly, over months and years, his gospel. Sometimes he slept there, since his students preferred he spend the night rather than try to find his way to one of their homes after dark. His eyesight had declined for years.

John shuffled up the grand street. His knees clicked painfully at each step. Occasionally he shaded his eyes, shading that had become easier, because he now walked bent over. He passed the bathhouse and plodded toward Rhianus' home.

Rhianus always told John that if he needed anything he was just to ask. Rhianus was more than a perfect host. He was a benefactor who didn't even request thanks. So this afternoon, when Rhianus stood waiting at the bottom of John's stairway, John was willing to do anything asked of him, which turned out to be a session of peacemaking between Rhianus' wife and her kitchen slave, who'd finally admitted to stealing three drachmas. The awareness of his painful joints and aching muscles melted away. All afternoon John, Rhianus, his wife, and her slave talked and prayed until everyone discerned that the Spirit of the risen Christ had settled the problem. As John became more and more aware of the risen Jesus' presence in their discussion, he lost his sense of time.

"We'll allow you to spend a few hours a week working in the neighbor's orchard," Rhianus' wife said to her slave. "You must repay what you've stolen and be trustworthy from now on in treating our possessions. Do you agree?"

The slave agreed.

"If you need more, talk to us. We'll work out something."

It was almost evening now as John, hands pushing down on each throbbing knee, mounted the stairs outside Rhianus' house. A few steps, then a rest. Was there any part of his body that wasn't tired? A few more steps, then a rest. He was relieved, finally, to enter his room. It was all he needed. He walked by the basin of water. He reached into the cabinet for his scroll. He looked longingly at the sleeping mat, but he walked by it to the cedar desk. He set the papyrus scroll beside the fresh ink and the sharpened writing reeds.

Fortunately, the room held two lamps and a large jar of oil. John realized that if he were to complete his writing task before sleeping, he must work well into the night. He cupped his hands over his eyes. Which were more exhausted — hands or eyes? He'd need both.

He sat down heavily in the purple chair that Rhianus had upholstered for him. He dragged the chair and himself up to the cedar table and from across it he pulled his gospel. The Christian community of Ephesus had pooled its money to purchase eleven papyrus rolls. As soon as John declared his work finished, his good news manuscript would be copied upon them and sent by messengers throughout the province and by boats across the sea.

His current version ended, accurately enough, "Now Jesus did many other signs in the presence of his disciples, which are not written in this book. But these are written so that you may come to believe that Jesus is the Messiah, the Son of God, and that through believing you may have life in his name." Because of the need of the Christian community in Ephesus, John was summoned by these very words to include one more of the many other things Jesus did. He now set about to append a further episode to his history of Jesus.

Years before, when John wrote his first words about Jesus' earthly ministry, his right hand, though still strong, shook with anxiety. Now, despite his age, he found from the first stroke of his reed that his hand was steady and his handwriting sharp and effortless.

He wrote of Jesus after his resurrection on Galilee's shore, and about the fish that morning on the boat's other side, and of Peter's splashing to the beach, and then Jesus' teaching Peter to care for the weakest believers. John concluded by recording carefully for his own anxious, frightened students what Jesus answered when Peter asked specifically about John. "When Peter saw him, he said to Jesus, 'Lord, what about him?' Jesus said to him, 'If it is my will that he remain until I come, what is that to you? Follow me!' So the rumor spread in the community that this disciple would not die. Yet, Jesus did not say to him that he would not die, but, 'If it is my will that he remain until I come, what is that to you?' "

Quickly, John scratched the words onto the papyrus roll. Relating Jesus' words in this scene inspired him as never before. He was compelled to write further: Even more important than what Jesus said about one follower is that Jesus is eternally the Lord. The risen Jesus is with us.

He wrote in a fury. Words leaped from his pen. Entire sentences formed at once. His very writing was an experience of the risen Jesus. How could anyone deny that Jesus has been raised from the dead, when his Spirit was so real and so pressing?

John felt his own spirit overflow with Jesus' presence, as if the Spirit of the living, resurrected Jesus surged through his pen. He had never been so certain of what he wrote: Jesus meets us at every corner we turn. He is present at every child's first gasping cry. He rejoices with the laughter at each wedding. Our unseen Lord accompanies us to our work and to the market. He is pleased with our successes and pained at our failures. He abides with us as we serve him with our youth and energy. He remains with us as we study about him and speak for him. When we read the holy scriptures, the risen Jesus leads us in our understanding. The curtain between earth and heaven flutters back and forth in the wind of Jesus' Spirit. God's life and our lives interpenetrate. We no longer know or care where one leaves off and another starts. He's with us to our last breath — and then, instantly, beyond.

John smiled to himself that he had finally completed this work for his risen Lord, but his is more than the joy of finishing: Jesus is with us because he loves us. Jesus promised, "I will not leave you orphaned; I am coming to you." His resurrection proves that we can't keep him out of this world. It makes no difference if he physically returns to earth before or after our death.

John's years dropped away as he wrote in ecstasy: Your life and Jesus' life are intertwined. He lives through you and you live in him. Today, this very evening, Jesus walks the streets of Ephesus with you. Can you see him? You might as well assume that he arrives at the harbor by boat. A boat stinking of fish. Just like the old days in Galilee. If you look for him now with your heart, you'll see him walking up the grand street. This night's darkness that slows and threatens us doesn't hinder him. He proceeds past the new marketplace's fragrant grain bins. He passes opposite the gaudy temple of Artemis. He pauses at the theater and listens to the actors throwing their lines.

You can trust that our invisible Lord visits our Christian gatherings tonight. He seeks out each believer. He wants to be with you, to strengthen, comfort, and instruct you. Wherever you are, Jesus comes to you. He'll find all who place hope in him. He further ascends the grand street and searches beside the bathhouse for where Rhianus lives. His message is always the same. I can hear him speak it. "I am coming to *you*." Surrounded by light, Jesus — even now — climbs the outside steps of Rhianus' house and enters the second-floor room with its cabinet of scrolls, sleeping mat, and purple chair. In the dim light of one lamp he comes upon a cedar table with fresh ink drying upon papyrus and a man, head down in death's sleep. The risen Jesus, his hand like a blessing upon the man's shoulder, nods his agreement to the manuscript's final words: "Jesus also did many other things. If each one were recorded, I suppose the world itself could not contain the books that would be written."

Discussion Questions

1. What immediate responses do you have to the story?

2. Do you identify with a character in the story? If yes, how and why do you identify with the person? If no, why don't you identify with anyone in the story?

3. Would you like to have a conversation with a character in the story? What would you say, ask, or suggest to the person? Why?

4. How does the story bring the biblical text into a clearer focus for you?

5. How would you improve or modify the story? Why?

6. Have you read the gospel of John and wondered how it was put together, especially its two "conclusions"?

7. Have you had an experience like John's, so close to the stories about Jesus that Jesus seems bodily present? How have you perceived the presence of the risen Jesus pressing upon you?

8. As John learned more about Jesus by living longer to reflect upon him, what is your newest understanding of Jesus?

9. What further depths of meaning, symbols, connections with, or applications of the biblical faith do you find in the story?

10. Since Jesus Christ has risen from the dead and is alive among us through his Holy Spirit, what of this story would you like Christ to activate in your life?

Emphasis or special occasion: Ordination

Chapter 27

The Seminarian

1 Corinthians 2:12

Albert Turner, in his third week of seminary, sat in a stuffy classroom in a boiling October heat wave wondering why he was there — morning until night studying Greek. At the blackboard Dr. Urbanski drew strange letters that Albert still could hardly name. He thought the words and diagramed sentences looked like a wiring diagram attempting to marry an algebra problem.

Doctor Urbanski said, "In the nominal system that includes, of course, adjectives as well as nouns, it is characteristic in the first declension that when the stem ends with a rho, case endings will all manifest a pure alpha, except, of course, in the genitive plural that is omega-nun in all declensions."

Albert turned to Dee opposite him. She was almost as confused as he was. She rolled her eyes and Albert smiled. Next to Dee, her roommate, Marilyn, was consumed in Dr. Urbanski's lecture. Dr. Urbanski, the great linguist, who, when he wasn't quibbling over how the author wrote the textbook, sometimes taught Greek. Marilyn took it all in. She walked around campus rattling off a series of nonsense syllables, then said, "Perfect, passive, indicative endings." Albert thought she and Dr. Urbanski might as well speak Martian.

"The use of case is slowly fading in the Koine/Hellenistic Greek, and is aided by the addition of prepositions. When grammatical structure employs only case for meaning, remember that the ablative is present in the form of the genitive, and, of course...."

Albert looked out the window. On the quadrangle, in a tree's shade, a mother was showing her child how to throw a ball so their Labrador retriever would bring it back. He glanced the other direction, over two rows to his roommate, Terry. Terry kept his handkerchief on his desk and regularly wiped sweat from his face and neck. Terry wasn't in the Marilyn-category of language geniuses, but he wasn't struggling as Albert was. Terry helped Albert every night, but in the end no one could learn for him. Why was he here? He thought God called him to be a pastor. His home church and pastor agreed. His parents were thrilled. All his life seemed to lead him to be a pastor; yet, he was unprepared for a month of intensive Greek. Nothing except Greek — lectures and tutorials, more lectures and tutorials, then evenings filling in a workbook, making flash cards, and trying to pronounce eight syllable words. Two doors down the hall from Greek class, second-year students studied Hebrew. Albert wanted to die, realizing a further perverse language awaited him.

"Be alert to the second/strong aorist person-number suffixes in the indicative mood that are identical with the imperfect person-number suffixes in the indicative. Of course, it is...."

As a preschooler, Albert played church with neighborhood children. He was the pastor, leading his favorite hymn, "Jesus Wears Glasses." He endured ups and downs in his faith — rebellion in junior high, doubts in high school — yet he never abandoned the faith or lost the sense that God had something for him to do. He believed God wanted him to be a pastor, knew that he liked and was capable of doing the things pastors did. However, his resolution sagged in the fall's early heat.

"Along with tomorrow's review of contract verbs, read the chapter on deponent verbs. That is six chapters ahead, but we shall study it out of the textbook's order. Greek deponents, of course, just like Latin deponents, have laid aside and lost their active form, and express the active voice through the middle or passive form. Bring your questions."

The students stood, their sweaty bodies released from sticky seats. Each began to collect their eleven pounds of books. Marilyn dashed up to Dr. Urbanski and engaged him in a scintillating conversation on prepositions. Albert, Dee, and Terry stood together. They looked at Marilyn, then looked at one another, shook their heads, and started back to their apartments.

"I don't know what deponent verbs are," Albert said. "But I think I am one. I'll bring myself tomorrow and throw myself onto Dr. Urbanski's desk, 'Here's a question that'll really stump you. Try answering me.'"

"You'll get it if you keep at it, Al," Terry said.

"I'm drowning, too," Dee said. "All I know is the difference between a noun and verb — in English!"

"Urbanski could do better," Albert said. "He's known this stuff so long he's forgotten how you learn it for the first time. He doesn't teach as though we're beginners, just stands there blabbering like a recorded textbook. 'Of course, of course, of course.' Well, of course, my horse! I don't know what he's talking about!"

That evening, Terry again helped Albert until late. Albert stayed awake long after Terry went to bed. He pronounced his way through paradigms and tried to remember the pattern of declensions. He picked up a stack of vocabulary cards, read a word in Greek, then tried to remember its meaning. He placed each card on his forehead to make it sink deeper into his mind. After little success he laid his head on the desk. He woke with saliva on his cheek and realized he'd slept over an hour. He shuffled to the bedroom in the dark, took off his shoes, and without changing clothes pulled a blanket over himself and fell asleep while trying to remember deponent verbs.

He dreamed the day over again: class — sweltering, stifling, and frustrating. Dr. Urbanski at the blackboard writing Greek words and pronouncing them in double gibberish. Then Jesus stood at the blackboard instead. Although Albert thought it strange that Jesus should be in class, Jesus acted quite at home. Chalk in one hand, eraser in the other, Jesus walked the aisles between desks, asking students to recite. Everyone could recite except Albert. He couldn't remember the present, active, indicative suffixes. Jesus stopped beside Albert and said, "You've been wondering if you should serve in the pastorate and if you should be in seminary learning Greek."

Jesus spoke a Greek word that Albert didn't recognize, "*Charizomai* to you your faith, as I have also your very life. You don't remember the Sunday school teacher in the nursery where your parents brought you at five weeks old. She and I were partners. I loved her. She loved all those babies for me. I shared your childhood and joined your parents' labor in raising you — whether you had colic or the croup, whether you passed or failed tests, whether you won or lost races. Remember when you played cops and robbers with Paco and Juan and the stick sliced you over the eyebrow? Nice scar! I was there to keep the stick from hitting your eye. You'd need your eyes for me. I arranged the world around you as certainly as your parents arranged the furniture in your house on Maple Street.

"You didn't see me standing in your classrooms, walking next to you as you delivered newspapers, or beside you when you cried for your lost dog. I was there because I promised I'd be." Jesus repeated the Greek verb, *"Charizomai* to you the starry nights at church camp that overwhelmed your soul. I was with you when you had your first kiss. I know, a real disappointment. I was with you when you fell in love. Because of me, you didn't marry Candice. As hard as that was, it wasn't just your or her decision, but my leading. And she's happy now.

"Charizomai your sins, and let you experience the release from guilt. I challenged you and comforted you at the right times. Albert, I'm your Savior. I'm also your Lord, and I know what I'm doing summoning you to seminary and planting you here in Greek class. You have every reason to understand how I've cared for you and guided you. Now trust me.

"Charizomai to you my ministry, instructing my people in faith, teaching them how to pray and trust, how to love and forgive. It's up to you to lead my church into my world so my concerns get beyond the borders of their own souls or families, churches or nations. They're my people and along with you I expect them to work for justice, peace, and harmony in my world. That's what you'll do as my pastor. It's the calling that perfectly fits who I created you to be.

"One thing more. *Charizomai* to you George Urbanski about whom you have thought and said such uncharitable things. He's granting you the benefit of 35 years of dedicated study to help you learn what my book means. And if you'd like to know, one night every week, in the clearest and simplest manner, he preaches at the rescue mission about my love for everyone, then he stays and washes dishes."

Albert could hear Dr. Urbanski washing the dishes. On and on it went, must be tons of dirty dishes, dishes everywhere, never knew there could be so many dishes. He wondered if he should help Dr. Urbanski. He opened his eyes to realize he was wearing his clothes in bed and Terry was in the kitchen washing the breakfast dishes. Albert, dazed and groggy, staggered out of the bedroom.

"Thought I'd let you sleep since you were up so late. If you want cereal, you've got a couple minutes to slug some down."

"I can't face breakfast. I'll get a candy bar at break."

They walked across the quadrangle together but Albert didn't speak. He stumbled along, rumpled and unshaven, half asleep, squinting against the morning sun, wondering about the dream. The dream remained as vivid as the fall leaves on campus.

He made his way to his seat, nodding hello to Dee and Marilyn. Dr. Urbanski entered and walked to the black board. Albert stared at Dr. Urbanski's hands to see how clean they were. "Deponent verbs. This morning I offer you a deponent verb that isn't covered in your text: *charizomai*. It is a word that well summarizes the entire New Testament message — the verb whose cognate noun means 'grace.' In the New Testament *charizomai* means, 'I grant you freely' or 'I grant as a favor.' It is also used in the phrase, 'I forgive or pardon sin.' You see why this one word is the essence of Christ's religion, the anchor of our faith, the motivation to love, and the best reason for hope. The endings are those of the present middle/passive indicative...."

Albert's eyes were as large as doorknobs. He felt dizzy: memories of childhood, suffixes for Greek verbs, fragments of his dream. However, he was alert enough to pray. He promised God to work harder to learn Greek. He had the presence of mind to thank God for his preparations to be a pastor. His life was all God's grace in Christ, even Greek class.

Discussion Questions

1. What immediate responses do you have to the story?

2. Do you identify with a character in the story? If yes, how and why do you identify with the person? If no, why don't you identify with anyone in the story?

3. Would you like to have a conversation with a character in the story? What would you say, ask, or suggest to the person? Why?

4. How does the story bring the biblical text into a clearer focus for you?

5. How would you improve or modify the story? Why?

6. What's the most difficult "training" that you've endured in order to serve God?

7. What is the most discouraged you've been in your attempt to live for God?

8. Has God ever seemed to break through to you with an important message or impression? In a dream? What were the long-term consequences?

9. What further depths of meaning, symbols, connections with, or applications of the biblical faith do you find in the story?

10. Since Jesus Christ has risen from the dead and is alive among us through his Holy Spirit, what of this story would you like Christ to activate in your life?

Emphasis or special occasion: Christian Ethics

Chapter 28

Setting: Corinth, Greece, 55 AD

1 Corinthians 8:1-13

The conversation paused as the slave, Rhoes, poured wine for the host and his reclining guests. In the silence, a ripple of wind from the Saronic Gulf stirred above their evening meal. One man began to talk but stopped. Another man coughed. A third man ran his fingers through his hair. The presence of Rhoes, the slave, made them uneasy. The nine had been hotly arguing as a group. They now began to chat among themselves in twos and threes. Two guests nodded to the slave and one even said, "Thank you, Rhoes." Although few looked directly at him, the slave, Rhoes, was the center of attention. The wine cups filled, the slave exited the opulent outdoor eating area, the nine men watching him as he left.

"Before we were interrupted," Lamprias, who was sitting farthest from the host spoke, "I was trying to explain that it's fine for our Christian gathering to include the likes of your slave here. In Christ there is no slave or free. But the slaves cause the most and the worst problems."

"Exactly," another said. "Did you see Rhoes eyeing the meat? He looked like he was leaning away from a hot kiln. I could almost hear him: 'I know where that meat came from.'"

"Brothers, brothers." A man lifted himself higher to speak. He had a narrow face and a thin, red beard. "We must explain again to Rhoes and his group that we believe in *one* God. That should be simple and sufficient. Stick with explaining about the one God and they're bound to catch the logic."

Quintus, nearest the host, said, "Along with that, we need a way to free the slaves — pardon the expression, Aristonicus." They all laughed, inclining their heads toward their host Aristonicus. "We need a way to free them from their fears of what they call gods."

"Thank you so much, Quintus," Aristonicus said. "Your suggestion for my financial ruin is duly noted." The men chuckled. "However, no one has devised a sure way to instruct our ignorant Christian brothers that God through Christ has already freed us all with the knowledge of salvation."

"I'm out of ideas of how to do it," one said.

"Me, too," an elderly man added. "On the Lord's day five weeks ago when we gathered at Aquila and Priscilla's house, I tried explaining to some slaves that no idol really exists and that they shouldn't criticize those who eat meat that's been slaughtered at a god's shrine. I told them that we also use the word 'god' to name evil spirits. To be precise, we should say 'so-called gods,' as we would if we were...."

He fell silent, and all nine glanced toward the slave, Rhoes, returning with a basket of bread.

"Of course I always bet on the Thracian," Quintus said to Aristonicus. "In the long races his horses always win."

"But that Cyprian has a strong stable this year," Aristonicus said. "He'll give the Egyptian *and* the Greeks a run for their money."

"Money? How much do you want to bet?" The discussion veered toward naming horses and owners and how many sesterces each man and his relatives had won or lost in the last three Isthmian Games.

Rhoes finished serving and left. After a moment, Lamprias said, "You'd think the slaves would be grateful that we're bound to them in the same faith and they'd admit we know much they don't. It's not because we open our houses for them to worship in. We, frankly, are more experienced in the love of wisdom and knowledge. I'd feel better if they at least asked me to explain to them something of the faith instead of cowering as they did when I pulled out the cold chicken I'd brought for the common meal."

"At least it wasn't pork," Quintus said and they laughed.

"That's another problem," someone said. "Let's leave the Jewish food superstitions out of it right now."

"But remember," the red-bearded man said, "this ultimately is a question about God. Is there one God and Father, from whom are all things and for whom we exist, and one Lord, Jesus Christ, through whom are all things and through whom we exist?"

"It's also about spreading the faith," Lamprias interrupted. "They can't ask us to sever all relationships with non-Christian friends and stop eating with them at their feasts. If Aristonicus had done that four years ago, the rest of us would never have become Christians."

They all agreed.

"Sure. Sure," the red-bearded man said louder, "but the chief issue is philosophical rather than practical. Is there one God or isn't there?"

Most of them nodded agreement. Then Aristonicus spoke. "Not just because Rhoes is my faithful slave, but in the fellowship of our Lord Jesus we must consider those who are weaker in knowledge and pray for them."

Quintus added, "No matter how irritating they are." The men laughed loudly. Their laughter carried to the kitchen where the slave, Rhoes, entered with his baskets. The slave, Kajul, stood awaiting his report.

"Yes," Rhoes said, shaking his head. "They're eating meat that was offered to idols and doing so as happily as Jews devouring the Passover lamb." He shivered. "I can hardly prepare that meat, let alone place it before them to eat."

"They're juggling burning sticks," Kajul said. "They're going to get burned. If anyone should know, I should. I paid dearly for continuing to eat in the temple of Askelpios."

"I remember the dreams you told me about," Rhoes said. "Demons ripping your flesh, plucking off your hands, eating your eyes."

"First thing, my goat died," Kajul said as he set aside a washed pot with a hard thump. "I know it was God's wrath because I didn't abandon my old life with a clean cut. Once I accepted Christ I stopped partaking of the meat at the shrines, but it was months before I finally gave up saving money by buying meat slaughtered at the temple — not until my wife miscarried. She's still pining."

"I also recall your child's face breaking out in sores. Ever think of that?"

"What bothers me most," Kajul said, "is that our master and his educated friends think they're invulnerable to evil. I can tell them what awaits their unfaithfulness, if only they'd listen."

"I mentioned to the master that you've been a Christian longer than he and that you could direct him upon the Christian path." Rhoes cut open pomegranates and placed them on a tray with apples. "But he says that in Christ we're free. He might know something about freedom, but we know about slavery."

"So we do," Kajul said, drawing a knife across his throat.

"And he's living in slavery," Rhoes said, "a continual slavery to the company of idolaters he enjoyed before he became a Christian. If he'd heed me, I'd tell him at least to stay clear of the temple area on public feast days."

"It's so simple," Kajul said, "yet the master makes it so complicated."

"Simple to us, but I'd say we are shackled in our attempt to instruct him. Wouldn't you?"

"Yes," Kajul said, smiling with resignation. "Pray for him. Don't let your disagreements tangle your feelings until you hate him. Pray for him. The master seems so strong and confident, but we know he's weak and we must pray for him and for his friends."

"I'm trying, Kajul," Rhoes said as he left the kitchen with his serving tray. "I'm trying. Pray for *me* as I serve beside their scraps of idolatry."

The young Christian church in Corinth is pockmarked with groups that discuss, gossip about, and accuse each another. The congregation is nearly drowning in its difficulties. Their painful problems have led them to write for advice to Paul, the apostle, their founding missionary. His first surviving letter to the Corinthian Christians responds to many of the disagreements they have mentioned. In this letter, Paul seldom agrees completely with any group. As he quotes their slogans, most of his responses are of the "yes, but" kind.

Once a week, about 100 Christians in Corinth meet at the home of Aquila and Priscilla, sharing an evening potluck in the atrium before sharing the Lord's Supper and listening to Christian teachers explain and apply their new faith.

The small Christian community is excited to gather and to hear Paul's precious letter to them; but when he writes, "Now concerning food sacrificed to idols," the ears of at least two clusters of people perk up. They listen even more intently. One group reasons, "Paul will admonish the immature that there's only one God and thus our diet, even eating meat from a temple restaurant, isn't central to our faith and therefore not a problem we must concern ourselves with." The other group thinks, "Surely Paul will rebuke the philosophical sophisticates who are staggering upon the cliffs of temptation, as they continue to devour meat offered in sacrifice at another god's temple."

Paul writes: "Now concerning food sacrificed to idols: we know that 'all of us possess knowledge.' Knowledge puffs up, but love builds up. Anyone who claims to know something does not yet have the necessary knowledge; but anyone who loves God is known by him.

"Hence, as to the eating of food offered to idols, we know that 'no idol in the world really exists,' and that 'there is no God but one.' Indeed, even though there may be so-called gods in heaven or on earth — as in fact there are many gods and many lords — yet for us there is one God, the Father, from whom are all things and for whom we exist, and one Lord, Jesus Christ, through whom are all things and through whom we exist.

"It is not everyone, however, who has this knowledge. Since some have become so accustomed to idols until now, they still think of the food they eat as food offered to an idol; and their conscience, being weak, is defiled. 'Food will not bring us close to God.' We are no worse off if we do not eat, and no better off if we do. But take care that this liberty of yours does not somehow become a stumbling block to the weak. For if others see you, who possess knowledge, eating in the temple of an idol, might they not, since their conscience is weak, be encouraged to the point of eating food sacrificed to idols? So by your knowledge those weak believers for whom Christ died are destroyed. But when you thus sin against members of your family, and wound their conscience when it is weak, you sin against Christ. Therefore, if food is a cause of their falling, I will never eat meat, so that I may not cause one of them to fall."

Paul proclaims that our behavior toward others cannot primarily be determined by our substantial Christian knowledge, our assured rights as free Christians, or even our spiritually illuminating experiences. Figuring out how to live for Christ isn't always simple; but, even when we disagree with others, our primary duty isn't to criticize them, correct them, or claim our rights despite them, but to love one another.

Discussion Questions

1. What immediate responses do you have to the story?

2. Do you identify with a character in the story? If yes, how and why do you identify with the person? If no, why don't you identify with anyone in the story?

3. Would you like to have a conversation with a character in the story? What would you say, ask, or suggest to the person? Why?

4. How does the story bring the biblical text into a clearer focus for you?

5. How would you improve or modify the story? Why?

6. As a Christian, have you been caught in a controversy similar to that in Corinth? What "side" were you on? Was it resolved or unresolved? As you reflect upon it from a later perspective, what could you (not someone you disagreed with, but you) have done in a more Christian manner?

7. Paul tells us specifics about how Christians should treat one another. Can you relate his instruction to a current controversy in the church?

8. What are Paul's main ethical principles in this passage and what other ethical principles need to be considered in order to have a balanced approach to Christian morality?

9. What further depths of meaning, symbols, connections with, or applications of the biblical faith do you find in the story?

10. Since Jesus Christ has risen from the dead and is alive among us through his Holy Spirit, what of this story would you like Christ to activate in your life?

Emphasis or special occasion: Church Conflict

Chapter 29

What A Rotten Text For Today

1 Corinthians 13

Note for reading aloud: The story is more convincing if two people read. One person reads the narration and the other is a middle-aged woman who reads what is printed in italics.

* * *

Esther Wright stood in front of the congregation with the Bible open before her. Her sweaty hands grasped the side of the lectern. She didn't know how she let things go so far. Usually, if she were angry or upset with anyone, even a church member, she would have settled it by now. But hers had been a full week: preparing flowers for two weddings (planned), and two funerals (unplanned), a friend in a bad car wreck, her son's basketball game out of town, and her first attempt at preparing the taxes for her own flower shop. Besides, she was just plain mad. She told herself a dozen times a day to drop it, but if she did drop it, she bent over, picked it up again, plunked it in her pocket, and by Sunday morning her pocket was beginning to smell pretty bad.

She'd waited too long. Yesterday afternoon at the shop she thought about it. By then the wedding flowers were safely in the brides' hands and the funeral flowers were wilting at the cemetery. She wasn't accomplishing anything more at work. Should have left right then, driven the eight miles to the Packen farm and tried to settle things with Linda — should have. Buford wouldn't have been a problem. He'd have been pleased for someone to confront his wife about her bullying. But Esther waited too long, and here she stood in front of the congregation on Sunday morning, her stomach complaining with cramps. Stuck in the middle of worship, her breathing was fast and shallow. Linda, Buford, and their kids sat in front of her in their usual pew.

Esther was repulsed with anger again. More than that, she was almost paralyzed. She had endured the first twenty minutes of worship, made some of the announcements, listened to the prayers, sang the hymns, and smiled through Pastor Bud's children's sermon. Now she must read from this large book before Pastor Bud preached. She'd led the congregation's worship often enough that she could read aloud and think at the same time. But she didn't like what she was thinking, nor could she halt her thoughts.

She thought, I wish the pastor had chosen one of the psalms that pray for vindication from our enemies. Or something from Joshua about God's armies wiping out the Canaanites. At least he could have chosen Jesus' telling his opponents they were whitewashed tombs.

She cleared her throat and read aloud Pastor Bud's large sticky note. *The reading this morning is from the apostle Paul's correspondence to the church at Corinth, the first extant letter, chapter 13.* She hoped this introduction would clear her head, let her distance herself from her emotions, push the problem out of the personal category so that, despite her gnawing feelings, she could pronounce the Bible's words for the congregation's sake.

It didn't work. She encountered the first words and nearly choked. *If I speak in the tongues of mortals and of angels, but do not have love, I am a noisy gong or a clanging cymbal.*

Her mind raced as she read. If Linda Packen could ever settle for someone else's opinion about how to decorate the church or about appropriate furnishings, this congregation's life would be infinitely easier. If she allowed perfection to be something less than her opinion, we'd get more sleep, take less ulcer medicine, and certainly see more people attend worship.

Esther gulped and pushed the next words through her teeth. *And if I have prophetic powers, and understand all mysteries and all knowledge, and if I have all faith, so as to remove mountains, but do not have love, I am nothing.*

In a fraction of a second, she reviewed the previous three weeks after the board had agreed with her decoration committee that the church building, inside and out, needed repainting. For all the people who said, "I'd like this color here or that color there," for all those who listened to one another, added suggestions, asked questions, even laughed with one another, not Linda. "The outside of the church needs to be white-white-white," she said. "Same color on the trim. White is the color God made village churches." She offered her declaration like Queen Victoria nodding from the throne.

Esther uttered the words of the next verse with her brain on autopilot. *If I give away all my possessions, and if I hand over my body so that I may boast, but do not have love, I gain nothing.*

Did anyone have more gall than Linda P? Esther's life and faith had been riddled with doubts and uncertainties. She faced enough problems from males who didn't want her in their business club, or, when she became a member, who dumped all the work on her. She had bushels of difficulties as Jeremy's single mom. How was it possible for someone like Linda P to enjoy perfect confidence that she was always right?

Esther hovered above the large print lectern Bible, her eyes dutifully making contact with the congregation. She extruded a few more syllables. *Love is patient; love is kind; love is not envious or boastful or arrogant or rude.*

Was there nothing she could do? Esther's week ruined, along with that of many other church members' weeks, by one person who always got her way. Nothing the congregation can do? Can a dab of paint never be dropped on a board or a drip of stain to a chair without passing through the fire of Linda P's non-debatable opinions? She even chose the design for the church letterhead, yet my degree is in graphic design! Has any church ever put up with such an attitude? Has a congregation existed that included such a person without losing half its members?

She heard her staccato words. *It does not insist on its own way; it is not irritable or resentful. It does not rejoice at wrongdoing, but rejoices in the truth.* What a rotten text for today. Pastor Bud had picked some obtuse scriptures before, showing a preference for Proverbs, James, and Chronicles, but this one made so many profoundly questionable statements. Esther had heard chapter 13 of 1 Corinthians read at weddings, but she usually was examining and critiquing the flower arrangements instead of listening. Now she thought that, in order to read it at a wedding, people had to be deranged. Their eyes and their thinking must have been glazed over. Has anyone honestly considered how dangerous Paul's advice is, such as, *It bears all things, believes all things, hopes all things, endures all things.*

Didn't Paul consider the consequences of what he suggests here? It's a license to let the wolves loose in the flock. It's a death sentence to fairness. Can't there be another way? Can't we be Christians and be strong, too? Can't we be Christians and stand for the right? Isn't our task also to point to human sin, describe it, and resist it? Can't we....

Love never ends, she read. *But as for prophecies, they will come to an end; as for tongues, they will cease; as for knowledge, it will come to an end.*

Esther shifted from one foot to another. If God is sending us into life's meat grinder, do we never defend against aggression, against the super-sized egos, against the hunger for power, not to mention disbelief? Must Christians just smile and take it, no matter what? Does God grant any guarantees that love will accomplish anything in the end? She let her thoughts mingle slightly with her reading, *For we know only in part, and we prophesy only in part; but when the complete comes, the partial will come to an end.*

So what is this, God, a test — having to look at Linda P's cherubic face, Linda P, who seems to have no awareness of how she grates upon everyone's patience, nor concern for those whose opinions she stomps upon? If I must undergo a test, I'd rather a pop-quiz on the tax codes for small businesses or even on color schemes for a convention of professional wrestlers. Or dump me on a deserted island with a Swiss army knife and a roll of duct tape and let me try to survive alone for a couple decades. But to face this woman is almost more than I can bear. I'd like to punch Linda P in the nose.

When I was a child, I spoke like a child, I thought like a child, I reasoned like a child; when I became an adult, I put an end to childish ways.

Esther's knees were shaking, her throat was dry, and those last words were hard to trip off her tongue. As were Paul's next sentences. *For now we see in a mirror, dimly, but then we will see face to face. Now I know only in part; then I will know fully, even as I have been fully known.*

What are we left with, the hope that something good will issue because we live Christ's way? You're asking a lot, God. Can I expect anyone in this congregation to wait for Linda P to change, although it has never seemed a possibility that Jesus' way of life will soon prove invincible? God, do you offer anything more, any qualifiers, any codas to compose on the end of your church's difficult song of obedience, a codicil to tack onto the advice you certify for your desperate servants? Do you have nothing more to recommend even in a church fight?

And now faith, hope, and love abide, these three; and the greatest of these is love.

Discussion Questions

1. What immediate responses do you have to the story?

2. Do you identify with a character in the story? If yes, how and why do you identify with the person? If no, why don't you identify with anyone in the story?

3. Would you like to have a conversation with a character in the story? What would you say, ask, or suggest to the person? Why?

4. How does the story bring the biblical text into a clearer focus for you?

5. How would you improve or modify the story? Why?

6. Without mentioning names or being too specific, what kind of conflict have you experienced in churches?

7. Have you been part of or witness to church conflict that was dealt with in a reasonable and Christian manner?

8. What is your style of handling conflict, especially in church? How does your style of handling conflict need to mature?

9. What further depths of meaning, symbols, connections with, or applications of the biblical faith do you find in the story?

10. Since Jesus Christ has risen from the dead and is alive among us through his Holy Spirit, what of this story would you like Christ to activate in your life?

Emphasis or special occasion: Faith

Chapter 30

Search For The True Believer

2 Corinthians 11:29

> Who is weak, and I do not feel their weakness? Who is led into sin, and I do not burn with indignation?
> — 2 Corinthians 11:29

Note: This is the author's translation.

* * *

Other than his family, in the last half of Ashley Settun's life, I knew him best. More people will speak about Ash at the banquet this evening, but I requested of the seminary's trustees, and they kindly granted me permission, to speak this morning. I'm pleased that so many of you, his former students, returned today, and I'm saddened that none of you current students knew Ash. I can tell you with absolute certainty he'd have wanted to know you.

I saw it so many times with first-year seminarians. We'd have our mixer at the beginning of fall semester to get students, staff, and teachers together over food. I observed new students encountering this skinny, bearded professor. No matter how nervous or brash they might be, within twenty minutes Ash was hearing their life story, asking them questions that plumbed their faith. In an hour, Professor Settun had another friend for life. Any of you have such an encounter with Ash? Ah, yes. No wonder so many of you are attending.

His nephew, Dwayne, who is a United Methodist pastor also, will say more tonight. But he agreed for me to relate that, when Ash's nephews and nieces were children, he asked them the same questions about faith and listened with the same attentiveness. Perhaps he viewed everyone, no matter their age, simply as God's children.

For you who weren't in touch with Ash after his retirement, I visited him almost every week in the last six years of his life. He was bedridden for much of his final eighteen months. Although Alzheimer's disease slowly pilfered his brain, Ash would give the perfect smile when I entered. I offered prayer or gave him a blessing before I left. Always as I'd leave, sometimes not until I was going out the door, he'd manage to say, "God bless you, too." It's taken another seven years since his death to organize and fundraise, and I'm grateful to the other committee members — all of whose names are printed in your program.

I've been asked to announce that the seminary store has for sale offprints of Ash's articles, recordings of his lectures and sermons, and half a dozen of his books. My advice to seminarians: Sell all you have and buy Settun's works. Your soul will profit as well as your mind — and your preaching. For the pastors present today, how many have preached Ash's sermons? Uh-huh. I won't ask if you gave him credit.

It never took long on campus for new students to learn that for money you went to Ash first. How many of you, when you repaid Ash, discovered he'd forgotten the loan? As executor of his will, I can tell you he was almost penniless at death. He'd long ago given away most of his possessions.

I expect more than anything you remember Ash's smile. Some people who didn't know him thought he was an idiot, walking across campus smiling — smiling at every person, smiling at squirrels, trees, wind, and sky. At first meeting he loved everyone; and thus, the truth that many didn't know, Ashley Settun's smile was also one of pain. Because of his love for God and others, he always wished he were a better Christian, a better human being, a better seminary professor. Because he never lived up to his standards, his life's pursuit was for someone who did. That, too, was part of his painful smile. He never found the true believer.

Everyone questioned by Ash faced his smile through which they experienced his acceptance and felt his empathy. His was a determined smile. Ash purposely and strenuously sought faith in others. He considered faith to be more mysterious than suffering. For all the quandaries we fall into, trying to understand, or worse, trying to explain this world's suffering — violent, senseless suffering of young or innocent — Ash was more enthralled, captured and held almost against his will, by the phenomenon of the Christian faith. Not: Why don't people believe, but why do they?

His smile, slightly sad, was the countenance of a human on a quest. He knew what he wanted. He was aware by its absence of what he sought. He wanted to identify a true believer. He searched for record of such people in arcane, dusty volumes in the library, in discussions with faculty and students, even in the high school Sunday school class he taught for 23 years. He was happy but not contented in his search. Of course, his own happiness wasn't his greatest concern. He wasn't consumed with self-interest, but with other-interest. He wanted to know the faith of other Christians. Basically, that was the theme of all he taught and wrote for forty years, no matter the title of the course, article, or book. His questioning of faith expanded to ask what it meant for a family to believe, for a community to believe, for a society to believe.

When I met Ash I was excited about my earning a Ph.D. in New Testament and being called to a seminary position. I was impressed with my doctorate. Ash wasn't. He wasn't impressed with my degree; he wasn't impressed with his. He just wanted to talk with people about faith: students, parishioners, or the needy people he met at the downtown mission, or in the mission in Guatemala he regularly visited.

I'm pleased to tell those who struggled here for years to learn enough Greek and Hebrew to barely pass the courses that Ash never learned Spanish well. He couldn't order a meal in Spanish without leaving the waiter chuckling. But no matter how foolish or offensive his Spanish, no one doubted his smile in any language. He reached out through the interpreter, "Tell me about your faith. How did you come to faith? What difference does faith make for you?"

Even when friends or relatives dragged him away from his work, got him off hiking, camping, or fishing, he'd be gazing at the natural world — not entering the endlessly unproductive and often disgraceful argument of creationism or evolution. Ash wanted to know what difference it made in a person to believe that this world was brought into being by the God and Father of our Lord Jesus Christ. To discover what difference faith made in our actual living, he interviewed people who set up charitable trusts or freely administered them. He spoke with parents of disabled children and parents who forgave their child's murderer. He questioned priests, police, and politicians. He interviewed Mother Teresa.

A colleague suggested he was turning theology into biography or anthropology. He answered, "I don't worship faith. I'm not defining God by people's experiences. I learn of God through Jesus Christ. I'm just profoundly interested in this facet of Christianity, as some professors are with church history or the biblical languages."

Now, Ash wasn't gullible. He could tell when someone used the word "faith" for what was really denial. He was aware of the faith that would collapse at the slightest problem. He discerned mere inherited faith from a struggled-for, or prayed-for, or studied-for faith. He knew enough of his own heart, and he'd talked with enough people, that he was fascinated by the possibility that a true believer existed. Has there been someone other than our Lord Jesus, is there someone, who has perfect faith? Someone whose life is directed by their facing toward God through all things, a person whose eyes, so to speak, are always on heaven, and who, therefore, lives on earth wholly by faith? Ash never lost hope that God could bring a person to complete faith. He never stopped searching for that individual.

So he met with faith healers. He attended all-night prayer meetings. He visited dying saints in the hospital, ghetto social workers, and pacifists who spent years in brutal prisons rather than agree to kill their fellow humans. One time I asked, "What would you do if you met him or her?"

"The true believer?"

"Yes."

"I'd ask them...." He looked over my head. "I'd ask them...." He looked higher above me, "to ... to bless me."

"That's all?"

"From a true believer? That would be enough."

Ten years into my teaching here, I was used up. I'd taught the classes my professors taught me (and done it better, I hoped), traced the ideas from my thesis into articles, and found myself, first, wondering what I was doing here, and, second, asking how I could ever stay in this profession. I was beyond glum. I don't know if I was clinically depressed. I didn't find out. I didn't even tell my wife these doubts about myself or of my calling, although she knew I'd changed. I hardly told God. I just agreed to another weekend's seminar, accepted the assignment to write another article, assented to serve on another faculty committee. I was as empty as our Lord's tomb, but with not an ounce of the joy that came from that vacated rock.

One day, after months of furious activity, I came to Ash's office and stood in the doorway. I was so numb I could barely speak.

"Come in and close the door." He motioned me to a chair. He smiled his painful, determined smile and waited. We sat staring at the carpet between us for five minutes. When I began to talk — all blubbering and confused — Ash hardly said anything for an hour. Then he asked, "Where did God begin with you?" And for another two hours, disregarding the phone and knocks at his door, he helped me walk back through my faith, follow backward the path that God had led me upon. Over the weeks and months that followed I began anew to discern God's purpose for me. After that I was never the same, but Ash was.

Especially, he was committed to our seminary's classes to rejuvenate pastors of declining churches. We offered similar classes for pastors of growing churches, because all pastors need spiritual help; but soon Ash wanted only to teach pastors of declining congregations, and certainly that was the majority of the mainline pastors who attended. Some for their entire careers pastored only declining congregations.

People thought that ministering to those pastors was his specialty. It wasn't. It's just that he found people there from whom he could receive as well as give. What kept them going? What beyond habit or loyalty to a denomination? What besides being without other skills and needing to support one's family? What held their faith together? Not: What doctrines did they hold? One could rattle off stuff memorized thirty years ago — whether understood or not. He wanted to hear in their own words how they saw themselves as children, or friends, or partners of the living God and thus why they lived in a godly way. Those pastors told him what their parishioners seldom asked or what their parishioners didn't want to know: the faith that sustained them even when members fled their congregation. When Ash heard such faith, he almost enfolded the pastor with his own spirit.

I've come to believe that Ash's relationship with each of his students was like that of the apostle Paul: "Who is weak, and I do not feel their weakness? Who is led into sin, and I do not burn with indignation?" If you studied with Ash, you see why I think that Paul's empathizing with people describes him. I think his faith in God was the same. God granted him a quality of openness not just to the struggles, concerns, and pains of others. This openness allowed him also to sense God's will and to yearn for God's interests.

I appreciate your attentiveness to this morning's introduction. I've been able to say things about Ash that I never said to him. I hope that everyone who wants to speak will have a chance at tonight's banquet, although that's dangerous with so many preachers on hand. Before the weekend is over, please add your memories to the book being prepared in Ash's honor. Again, on behalf of the seminary's trustees, faculty, administration, and student body, I welcome you to this weekend of celebration. It was my privilege to know Ash as a colleague and friend. It's an equal privilege now to dedicate this endowed professorship for the study of the Christian faith in the name of Ashley Settun, a true believer.

Discussion Questions

1. What immediate responses do you have to the story?

2. Do you identify with a character in the story? If yes, how and why do you identify with the person? If no, why don't you identify with anyone in the story?

3. Would you like to have a conversation with a character in the story? What would you say, ask, or suggest to the person? Why?

4. How does the story bring the biblical text into a clearer focus for you?

5. How would you improve or modify the story? Why?

6. How did you come to faith? Has your faith been like a struggle, journey, or surrender?

7. As you trace backward the path upon which God has led you, where do you see God helping your faith most?

8. How have other people helped your faith? Has one person for you been an excellent example of faith? How have you helped others in faith?

9. What further depths of meaning, symbols, connections with, or applications of the biblical faith do you find in the story?

10. Since Jesus Christ has risen from the dead and is alive among us through his Holy Spirit, what of this story would you like Christ to activate in your life?

*Emphasis or special occasion: Thanksgiving or
Martin Luther King Day*

Chapter 31

Languishing Legend

Galatians 3:28

Perhaps once, if you're fortunate, you'll meet a legend. My once was October 2006. I'd flown from Bozeman to Seattle for a seminar that proved to be neither relevant nor interesting, and not just for me. More people were sleeping on their notebooks than listening to the presenter. Half a dozen of us decided at lunch that if the afternoon session wasn't better we'd leave early and head to the waterfront for some of Puget Sound's famous fish.

At the 3:30 break, the six of us just looked at one another, gathered our notebooks and handouts, and left the conference room. We agreed to gather at 4:30 in the lobby, but by five o'clock one fellow was still waiting for a call back from his office, another didn't feel well, and another didn't show up and didn't answer when we rang his room. Of the other two, I didn't know one and didn't have anything in common with the other, so I begged off, too. Still, I wasn't about to attend the evening session.

I phoned home and talked with my wife, Starla, and chattered with Joshua about school and spoke Amy's name and heard her giggle in the receiver. Starla said, "Your mom phoned. Nothing special. Just to talk."

So I phoned my mother in Yakima and told her what happened to my Seattle evening. She said, "Why don't you phone Jenny?"

"Who?" I said, trying to divert her, though I knew who she was talking about.

"Cousin Jenny Wilson. She lives in Seattle."

"Mother, I don't know Jenny Wilson."

"You'd love her. She's the Jenny who told off Uncle Roscoe."

"I remember."

"She'd be thrilled to have you phone. She's our only family in western Washington. No other family near her."

"Mother, I don't know."

"Please. I'd like you to call her. I feel guilty. I haven't seen her for years. I plan, but something always comes up. She was very good to your grandparents."

Before I could say more, mother was thumbing through her address book, commenting upon people whose names she passed. Evelyn Dupree had been in the hospital again. Audrey and Leon Kelfer were already snowbirding in Arizona. Nola and Owen's daughter was getting married for the second time — to an architect. Then she gave me Jenny Wilson's phone number.

She was pleased. I ended the conversation miserable. An evening of boring lecture with substandard visuals sounded better all the time. But I'd never won an argument with my mother. For that matter, I don't remember ever winning an argument with any female in my mother's family. Call it an argument, a disagreement, or simply a debate, even if I survived the discussion, thinking I'd made really good points, they always walked away as though they won.

A woman's voice answered. I asked, "Is this Jenny Wilson?"

"Yes."

"My name is James Stroud, your cousin, Maxine's, son."

"Oh, yes. Hello, James."

"I'm in Seattle for a seminar and Mother suggested I phone you." I didn't mention a dinner. Dinner with a stranger significantly older than my mother didn't compare well with an evening with peers joking about our bosses.

"That's nice," she said. "Let's see. I'm trying to match some event in my life with news of your birth so I can remember your age."

I hesitated. Mother never freely admitted her age. I guess I'd caught that from her. I said, "I'm 32."

"My, I wouldn't have guessed it. Although that stands to reason. You're married."

"Yes. Starla and I've been married eight years."

"And children?"

"Uh-huh. Joshua's in first grade and Amy's nineteen months."

"That sounds like a fine family."

A pause. She didn't seem like the kind of old person who only talked and didn't listen. I said, "I have the evening off and wondered if you'd go to dinner with me. Get the family together, if only two at a time."

"Wonderful. Where do you want to eat and when?"

"I was thinking about Ivar's Acres of Clams on the waterfront. I've heard it's good."

"It's excellent."

"I could pick you up in an hour. I've rented a car."

"Thank you, no. That's okay. I'll take a taxi."

"But I've got a car."

"Thank you, but meeting you there is fine. What time?"

I realized that by telephone I'd just met another female in my mother's family and immediately she got her way — which felt something like my losing an argument, disagreement, or simply a debate. We agreed to meet in an hour. I phoned for a reservation and rushed to make sure I arrived early.

Ivar's was easy to find on Pier 56. I enjoyed the smell of the saltwater and kelp as I walked along the waterfront in the mild October evening. Outside the restaurant I heard people discussing Seattle's drought: nine days without rain.

I sat in the booth waiting for Jenny and tried to remember what Mother had told me about her. She'd never married and was a big-wig attorney, specializing in trade with Asia, long before women normally had such careers. Most of what I remembered was Mother's recalling the clash with my great-uncle, Roscoe — a person I met once as a child. I vaguely remember a man with fluffy mutton-chop sideburns and dozens of blood vessels veining his cheeks. I think he gave me peppermint candy.

The first time Mother told Tim, Donna, and me about the confrontation was our first Thanksgiving dinner after Father died. "We must remember the good things about Father." She was wrong. What could any of us remember then that wasn't painful? We'd need such things later, but right then, trying to talk about Father wasn't working.

Mother was filling our plates. We three kids were silent. She tried again, "If we each share one good memory...." I noticed the desperate sound in Mother's voice and the tears forming in her eyes. I was oldest. I felt responsible, but I didn't know what to do or say. She hesitated, holding a gravy boat.

"I don't think ... I don't remember if I've told you about Cousin Jenny Wilson."

She put down one plate and grabbed another, and doing so, she was past her ragged beginning. She found her pace by telling us of Jenny, just as she found her pace when she sewed. She'd take a few choppy beginnings at a seam on the sewing machine, then crush her foot on the foot-feed and off she'd go, almost without a break. She was now engaged in the subject of Cousin Jenny.

"When I was home from college for Thanksgiving — senior year 1966 — the Civil Rights Movement was well underway. Civil rights means you can't treat people differently because of their color or religion or such. Civil rights means that every person truly is equal by law to every other. But then in the United States quite a few whites resisted the belief."

She finished filling Donna's plate and sat down. "I hadn't anticipated that Thanksgiving being different than any other, and it wouldn't have been, if Roscoe had kept quiet. The meal was at your grandparents' in Yakima about three in the afternoon. Small family gatherings were always in the evenings; large events were mid-afternoon. Family had been arriving since noon from all over the state — small children playing upstairs, teenage boys outside throwing the football to one another, and often throwing it at the teenage girls huddled on the front porch. Some of the older girls helped the women cook. Men sat in the living room. I felt halfway between a teenager and an adult because I was still in college, but I took my place in the kitchen with the women.

"When Cousin Jenny came, however, she sat in the living room with the men. Jenny was fifteen years older than I. The noise level in the living room plunged when she arrived. Jenny wasn't only a woman, but an educated woman. She started college at the end of

World War II and attended a school that taught both Japanese and German because she planned to make some impact for good for America's recent enemies. Now she regularly crossed the United States and the Pacific. She was, as my father said, nobody's fool.

"After a couple of my trips to the table, the men talked loudly again and then Roscoe was shouting. I stuck my head around the corner. He stood, face red, veins on his temple pulsing, and pointing at Jenny. Mother ran by me and dashed over to him. He was her brother. Square in front of him with her hands on her hips, she said, 'None of your shouting in my house.'

"He quieted, but the other men in the room either grinned because Roscoe so clearly was bested by a young woman, or grimaced, knowing that Roscoe would certainly pop off again, probably during dinner.

"Our dinner seating looked like a crossword puzzle, all the tables in the house and a couple borrowed card tables pushed together. Family stretched from the dining room into the living room. Fifteen minutes after the meal started Roscoe raised a ruckus. Hard to tell exactly what was going on. But as everyone hushed, Roscoe sneered at Jenny, 'I suppose you heard that from Liver-Lip King *JUNior*.'

"Jenny's jaw was set as tightly as a miser's cash box. She merely uttered, 'No.'

" 'Oh, really! You're not spouting propaganda from Fartin' Luther King?'

" 'No.'

" 'Well then, where you get all these uppity ideas? From your law schools' liberal professors?'

" 'No.'

" 'Come on, come on. You want to change the way the world's always been. Where you scavenging your thoughts? Who's pumping sewage into the public's brain now?'

"This time Jenny didn't answer. Roscoe obviously thought her silence meant his questions had overpowered her opinions. He huffed up his chest: 'Where you hear such things, girl?'

"Jenny glanced slowly to her left and right and saw that everyone was looking at her. Surely she knew that everyone hoped she'd knock Uncle Roscoe down to size. Very slowly and clearly she said, 'The Bible.'

" 'Ha!' he said. 'Everybody quotes the Bible, but *where*? Where's the Bible say blacks are as good as whites?'

" 'There is neither Jew nor Greek, there is neither slave nor free, there is neither male nor female; for you are all one in Christ Jesus.' Galatians, chapter 3, verse 28. Now, you tell me where the Bible says that other races are inferior to whites.'

"Uncle Roscoe glared at her and was opening his mouth when your grandfather said, 'Yeah, Roscoe, tell us.' Then someone else said, 'Sure, Roscoe, preach the Bible for us.' Then a couple people sniggered and pretty soon everybody was laughing at Roscoe. He didn't sit. Just stomped out. Your grandmother said he didn't return to a family gathering for four or five years."

I sat in the Seattle dusk remembering how Mother first told us of that Thanksgiving tiff between Roscoe and my cousin, Jenny. It became a favorite of us three children. Even into adulthood, when we gathered for Thanksgiving, one of us would ask Mother to recite Jenny's triumph. Jenny was a legend, and although I'd seen photos of her, in my imagination I pictured her as a kind of female Theodore Roosevelt, and always heard her say things like, "Free at last, free at last —"

"James?"

I wasn't prepared to look up and see a thin, wispy-haired lady with tiny, crooked fingers curled over a cane. I suppressed my surprise. "Jenny?"

She gave me a beautiful smile and we carefully shook hands. "Please, sit down," I said. She balanced her cane upon her lap, and by shuffling slowly she managed to be seated next to the window.

"I'm really glad you could make it," I said. I tried not to gawk at her feeble, twisted body and arthritic fingers.

"I don't go out often," she said as she put her napkin on her lap. We ordered and it took only a few minutes into the meal to finish the same kind of information we'd covered on the phone: wife, children, job, home, all the basics. Jenny told me she'd been retired for eleven years. "I don't do much anymore. I only get out to church. Other than that I head the church's prayer chain and phone volunteers to donate blood." She smiled weakly. "Mainly, I languish."

With that, Jenny didn't say much more. We ate politely. She often gazed out the window at Puget Sound. The October sun was almost down, turning her a reddish orange. I was struck by how the autumn sun colored this distant cousin of mine. She was so courteous and seemed super-intelligent. She was also sorrowful. Even nature seemed to paint her sad with an autumn sunset.

"Well, Jenny," I said, "it seems like you do quite a bit."

"It's almost nothing." She choked a little on her food. "Quite a step down from international joint ventures. It's almost nothing, but that's all I can do anymore: almost nothing."

"All you can do is all you can do." I tried to look wise while I mouthed such a stupid cliché.

"Maybe, but there's not much joy in being able to do so little. I hope you don't have to grow old as I have — wearing out piece-by-piece and finding less and less even to look back on with any sense of accomplishment."

She stared off toward the setting sun. It seemed to be sliding the last eighth of an inch below the horizon.

"You know, Jenny, I never met you, but I heard about you."

"Your mother is such a dear."

"Yeah. She's superb. And she always talked about you and of your run-in with Roscoe at Thanksgiving 1966."

"1966, was it? I remember Roscoe! I think if he were here he'd trip me with my own cane."

"It was the Thanksgiving after Father died when Mother first told us about your spat with Roscoe."

Jenny shifted fully toward me instead of partially facing the window.

"I think she decided we needed to learn something important that day. She was determined to give us something significant, if not as important as having a father, something meaningful anyway. Over Thanksgiving dinner she told us of you and Roscoe, and the Bible and Martin Luther King Jr. and what he tried to do for our country.

"She repeated it every Thanksgiving after that. When I was older I read Doctor King's writings. At Thanksgiving I talk about Martin Luther King Jr., and what he meant to our country. The rhythm of his sentences are in my heart. The meaning of his words are in my bloodstream. They've made me who I am, and thus you've helped make me who I am."

Jenny's head was shaking slightly, the autumn sun glowing behind her free strands of hair.

"I'm passing this onto my children. When we talk with Joshua about what it means to be a Christian, I instruct him how to resist evil with good. I tell him how Doctor King promised whites that his people would still love them, no matter what whites did to them.

" 'We shall match your capacity to inflict suffering by our capacity to endure suffering. We shall meet your physical force with soul force. Do to us what you will and we will still love you ... But be assured that we'll wear you down by our capacity to suffer, and one day we will win our freedom. We will not only win freedom for ourselves; we will so appeal to your heart and conscience that we will win you in the process, and our victory will be a double victory.' "[1]

"I, I ..." Jenny said. "I had no idea. Roscoe and I ... That was so long ago."

"Not to me," I said.

She reached across the table with her small, bent fingers and we held hands for a moment.

"Thank you," she said.

After dinner I had a cab called for her. By then the wind was blowing across the sound. It wasn't wise for her to be outside long. She gave me a little hug and told me she appreciated the evening. She tottered to the taxi, then she was gone. I leaned into the October wind and watched her taxi until it was out of sight. I scuffed along the sidewalk and hummed for a time. The wind flapped my pant legs. I looked in the direction the taxi had gone and I gazed upon the final pink of the sunset. It's not as though the evening was the magnitude of Jacob's wrestling with the angel, but I finally won a verbal contest with a female of my mother's clan, and it was a deep and a double victory.

1. Martin Luther King Jr., *The Trumpet of Conscience* (New York: Harper and Row, 1967), pp. 74-75.

Discussion Questions

1. What immediate responses do you have to the story?

2. Do you identify with a character in the story? If yes, how and why do you identify with the person? If no, why don't you identify with anyone in the story?

3. Would you like to have a conversation with a character in the story? What would you say, ask, or suggest to the person? Why?

4. How does the story bring the biblical text into a clearer focus for you?

5. How would you improve or modify the story? Why?

6. Do your rituals at Thanksgiving or other holidays involve telling family legends?

7. Have you had the experience of thanking a person for what their life has meant to you? Has anyone thanked you for what your life has meant to them?

8. Do you remember when you first heard of the Civil Rights Movement and Doctor King's work? What did you think of civil rights then? What do you think of civil rights now?

9. What further depths of meaning, symbols, connections with, or applications of the biblical faith do you find in the story?

10. Since Jesus Christ has risen from the dead and is alive among us through his Holy Spirit, what of this story would you like Christ to activate in your life?

Emphasis or special occasion: Father's Day

Chapter 32

How Are Things In Guanajuato?

Ephesians 3:14-19

As a young girl, Father's Day didn't bother Sarah as much as school events: concerts and plays. Her friends looked in the stands to spot their mothers and fathers. Sarah didn't have a father. After repeated requests, her mother once uttered her father's name. Sarah would never hear it again. "Duane Lumen." Her grandmother, with whom they lived, never spoke his name, but a half dozen times she responded to Sarah's questions, "He chose the silver mines of Gwanawata," a word she almost spit, "to being a father." A couple times when her grandmother was in such a mood, Sarah tried her rhymes, "Oh, Grandmother, bandmother, landmother," but she couldn't win a smile.

Sarah was ten when she realized that her grandmother said nothing good about anyone. She was a teenager when she first guessed that her mother's sadness was caused as much by her grandmother as by her father's leaving.

During freshman year at Southern Oregon University, Sarah stumbled when she saw the street sign, "Guanajuato Way." She discovered that Guanajuato was Ashland's sister city and the university had an extension there.

She called it: "The convention of a Mexican extension."

She stretched further: "For your retention," but it didn't work.

In her first two years at the university, she offered friends to the tune of "How Are Things In Glocca Morra?" her rendition: "How are things in Guanajuato? Are the silver mines producing there?"

She added other lines, "Does silver still from campfires flow?" And "Are mestizos still exploited there?" But her friends hadn't read about Guanajuato and didn't know the tune, not having been forced as children to watch the *Lawrence Welk Show* with their grandmother.

Sarah couldn't recall exactly when the idea of studying her junior year in Guanajuato entered her mind. Thus, it was as if it had always been there and she never doubted she wanted to go. She dreaded telling her mother. She thought of sending a letter: "Dear Mom, here's the bomb: I want to go to Gwana-wha-toe."

She decided on a more prosaic, and oral, announcement. Yet, after her third visit home to talk with her mother about it and receiving only negative answers and reasons, Sarah said, "I really want to do this and I'm the one who'll have to pay for the loans."

Her mother tightened her lips, squinted her eyes, and nodded her head yes. Her grandmother, on the other hand....

Three weeks after arriving in Mexico's old colonial capital, she began every Saturday morning taking the bus uphill to the Valenciana silver mines. She asked anyone near or outside the mines, "Do you know Duane Lumen?" Usually the men didn't answer, although she was certain they could understand her, no matter her accent.

A month's practice of this exercise and she now said, "Have you met an American named Duane Lumen?" The one mine official who spoke to her offered no help and watched her as though she were recruiting his workers or stealing his silver.

On her fifth Saturday at the mine, a man waited at the bus stop. He was six feet, bent, and his right shirt-sleeve was safety pinned onto his shoulder for lack of an arm. When she stepped from the bus he walked toward her, slightly dragging his right foot. He appeared at least fifty. He smiled and spoke native English, "Are you the girl asking about Duane Lumen?"

She was startled at the name and hesitated to respond. She'd heard the name spoken only once by another person and it had sounded angry. "Yes," she finally said.

"I was with him when he died."

She wasn't over the surprise of someone's speaking her father's name, and now the further shock that he was dead. She looked up at the man but couldn't manage a word. His face that had seemed friendly began to show irritation.

"Many men still die in these mines, even Gringo engineers."

"No," she said, "that's not it. I, uh —"

"Well, you asked about Duane. What is it?"

Sarah spoke slowly, expressing what in twenty years she'd never said aloud, "Duane Lumen was my father."

The man's eyes became wide and he said, as though answering a question, "You're ... you're Sarah." He stepped forward as if to hug her, then stopped and offered his left hand. "I'm Tony Deford. I had to stop and listen to my memory to hear Duane say your name."

"I want to know about my dad."

"Well, come on in."

They entered a building that was terraced into the hillside. They ascended an unlit staircase. Tony stopped at a landing, kicked aside a newspaper, and bent down to warn her about where scorpions usually hid. He guided her up another flight. "We don't usually work Saturdays; but even if the place were full, no one's been here long enough to know your dad."

The room they entered was lit by one window whose dirt filtered light to an orange glow. As they sat on leather *equipales* chairs, dust puffed up around them. Sarah told Tony that she was studying at the university and that she'd learned of Guanajuato in Ashland, Oregon.

"I don't remember my father and I didn't know he was dead."

Tony's jaw fell, "Your mother didn't tell you?"

"Mom said he left and never came back. That's what Grandma said, too."

"The boss wrote your mother and sent Duane's belongings. I dictated a letter to go with it while I was in the hospital. It could've been stolen in the mail. If she thought he'd left for good, that might explain why she didn't inquire about him."

"Probably," Sarah said. "What do you know about Dad? Anything you can tell me is more than I know."

"Your dad and I came here about the same time." Tony leaned back and made his chair squeak. "I'd worked in Mexico six or seven years. He came straight from the States. Attended mining college somewhere — Texas A&M? Didn't graduate, but Duane was a smart fellow, hard worker. He mentioned you and that he was saving to go back north and make a good home for you."

Sarah managed to ask, "And you worked together a lot?"

"No, we weren't always with the same crew; but as the only Americans we were birds of a feather on weekends. I expect now that I've opened my memory's door some things about your dad will wander out. You coming up here again next Saturday?"

"I can."

"Then I'll dig around at home and see if he's in one of the shift pictures."

"You and Dad started together?"

"Same year, anyway. Right off — and I'm sure this is what Duane would want you to know — is that he walked over to Valenciana's gold-gilded church. He knew enough Spanish to figure out it was built by the blood of the miners. Neither of us liked that. We didn't really know what we were doing, but we started going to a small Protestant church in Guanajuato. We talked about it a couple times — faith and God. Neither of us went to church as children. I didn't have a mother. He didn't have a father. Pretty messed up childhoods, and marriages, too, to tell the truth. He never said it exactly, but he came to work in Guanajuato to get his life together."

Tony paused and looked at the floor. Sarah dabbed her eye with a tissue. "We were in church together that Sunday and in the mine Tuesday. No," Tony shook his head and closed his eyes, "Wednesday. We were with a group of six on an inspection when a cave-in caught us. I was right next to him. I deposited my arm there," he pointed to his right shoulder, "as a memento. Everyone coughed in the dust that surrounded us like a hot, black mist. A couple guys started tossing rocks off me. Duane's legs were crushed and his torso trapped. Nothing they could do for him. I was pretty bad off and men were yanking on me. We were about a foot apart. He looked me in the face and said through his gasps, 'I'm going to see my father.' I was hurting so bad I couldn't speak. Hardly conscious. Then he said — I swear this is what he said — very clearly, 'and my heavenly Father.'"

Tony sat silently as Sarah stared red-eyed at the wall, swallowing hard a couple times. He asked her what subjects she was studying at the university, then he took her to lunch, which stretched out for two hours. He asked many questions about the last two decades in the US. As they discussed Sarah's plans after college, they found they both liked Faulkner's novels, Frost's poetry, and big band music.

The next Saturday, Tony brought a wrinkled eight-by-ten photograph of day shift. He pointed to Duane Lumen and Sarah gazed at it with her mouth open. "You can have it," Tony said. He pointed, "And that fellow with two arms and not a lot of sense is me." Sarah laughed, then she cried.

Tony led Sarah to the cemetery. He left her alone at her father's grave and he wandered away to sit on a tombstone beside a marble angel. After their visiting the cemetery, they went for another long lunch. They spent an hour reciting their favorite poems.

"If you'd like to," Tony said, "I could come down to Guanajuato next Saturday to meet you for lunch." When they parted he hugged her and Sarah experienced that a hug with one arm was as satisfying as with two. She looked out the bus window and waved again to Tony.

She looked at the beat-up photograph on her lap. She would never discover why news of her father's death hadn't reached her family. But her father believed he would see his father and his heavenly Father.

She lost a father she never knew. However, Tony didn't have a family and they both had Saturdays free and much yet to be discussed about Faulkner's *As I Lay Dying* and about snowy roads not taken.

As the bus bounced downhill, she jotted a few words on paper, starting a letter to her mother. The tune of "How Are Things In Glocca Morra?" popped into her mind and she started humming her own lyrics. For a few days, at least, she would wait and think about exactly how to tell her mother about her father's death. For now, Sarah hummed her song quietly to herself, "Things are well in Guanajuato, this fine day."

Discussion Questions

1. What immediate responses do you have to the story?

2. Do you identify with a character in the story? If yes, how and why do you identify with the person? If no, why don't you identify with anyone in the story?

3. Would you like to have a conversation with a character in the story? What would you say, ask, or suggest to the person? Why?

4. How does the story bring the biblical text into a clearer focus for you?

5. How would you improve or modify the story? Why?

6. Did you know your father? Did your father contribute to your faith? If you didn't know your father, how did that affect your faith?

7. Has someone in your life been like a parent to you? Do you have someone to whom you are like a parent?

8. Does the image of God as Father help or hinder your faith? Does it offend you or help you to speak of God as Parent or as Father/Mother?

9. What further depths of meaning, symbols, connections with, or applications of the biblical faith do you find in the story?

10. Since Jesus Christ has risen from the dead and is alive among us through his Holy Spirit, what of this story would you like Christ to activate in your life?

Emphasis or special occasion: Football

Chapter 33

Team Bus

Ephesians 4:15-16

Dear Pop,
   In this last month, especially since it's football season, I've thought a lot about our conversation. I can't excuse myself by saying I knew what I meant but didn't say it correctly. I wasn't clear in my own mind when I said that football had taught me Christian morality. You said that Jesus wouldn't teach youngsters to bash one another. I'm sorry I said that he'd probably teach them to make a mortise and tenon joint.
   I had one aspect of football, or I should say specific coaches and a definite situation, in mind when I said there were other ways to learn it, yet I did learn the balance of Christian morality through football. Because I gained so much through football, I quite unconsciously call everyone who teaches or directs me "coach." I've even called you coach, though such a title isn't usual for one's father-in-law, let alone for a Mennonite pastor.
   I can't go as far as you in calling football players "thugs with helmets," especially since I wore one of those helmets for eight years through high school and college. I grant that your observation of the game as a boot camp for civilized war and the players as apprentice soldiers isn't completely wrong. And I agree that, as there is no Christian war, so there is no Christian football game. I agree it's blasphemy to break limbs, warp lives, and maim children. And, yes, I agree athletics has been exalted to a religion in America.
   Since it was my game, I can tell you more. I have experienced football fans as bloodthirsty, like car-racing enthusiasts hoping for a wreck. I've seen whole communities creating an excuse to hate

the fans sitting in the opposite bleachers. Beyond your observations, again since it's my game, I've found it a hoax that football builds character. It's like saying that studying chemistry builds character. Morally, football ranks with jousting. It's just that, whichever way in life football players choose, they will probably have more physical strength and more mental discipline to advance in that direction — whether for good or bad.

Yet, there's much I didn't tell you, things I hardly understood it myself. Beyond the violence and the obvious goal of physically beating the other team, there's more. It's not visible on the field or written in the record books, but it's in my memory and in my life. It's complicated and has taken me years to unravel, scrutinize, and comprehend. And believe me, the understanding has been accelerated this last month; because, not only do I take your opinion seriously, but I respect and love you as my own father. So, Pop, this is my fuller explanation as I've formed it during some sleepless nights over the last weeks.

When I said football taught me balance in Christian morality, I was speaking about one night during football season in my high school senior year. It wasn't at a game, but after; and it didn't really start that night, but seventeen years earlier. We'd played Elias, which lay on the other end of the conference. Our team stopped for a fast-food meal on the outskirts of Elias, and by 10:30 p.m. we were on the bus starting our three hours of bouncing toward home.

We'd won the game, but not by much, and Elias hadn't only gained more yards than we had, they'd basically beaten us everywhere except on the scoreboard. So we traveled home relieved, but not overjoyed. Some of the guys slept, a couple groups played cards, and clumps of fellows talked and joked.

Warren and I sat near Coach Sanders and Coach Cronin. It worked that way on our team. The older you were, the nearer you sat to the coaches, because they usually debriefed the team's performance with the seniors and talked about moves in personnel or strategy for the next game. That night they sat third seat from the front, left side, Coach Sanders by the window.

Contrary to the rides home from other games, even from losing games, the coaches spoke little, to the seniors or to one another. They sat rigidly in the dark, and we who were near them felt anxious with their silence.

Coach Cronin looked like a football player. In high school and college at defensive tackle and offensive guard his nose was broken three times. He walked like a bear and had a voice you could hear a half mile away. Yet he had tiny smooth hands and he'd walk around in the locker room and gently pat the players on the shoulder pads.

Charles McBride, our star receiver, dropped two passes in the first quarter of the game with Barrett. At halftime Cronin bent over to talk to him, but Charles wouldn't raise his head, just sat there, looking at the floor. Cronin got on his knees and looked up into Charles's face, whispering to him while he held both small hands on Charles's shoulders. No matter how badly a boy had performed in practice or in a game, Coach Cronin laid his tiny hand upon his head or shoulder and quietly encouraged him, almost begging him to do better. Warren said he wished Cronin wouldn't do that. He'd rather he'd yell and cuss at us, because when Coach Cronin said that you could do better and that he wanted you to try harder, you certainly would, but first you wanted to cry for ten minutes.

Coach Sanders was tall and heavy and had played wide receiver. His face was like a cherub's. You'd meet him walking alone in the hall, humming to himself and smiling, and you'd feel as though the world was spinning on its correct axis. Warren said that a photo of Coach Sanders could win your vote or convince you to invest your life savings in his bank. Sanders had a shrill, thin voice, almost like a bird. Sanders would scream at us that we were sissies, that we played like ballet dancers — girl ballet dancers. He said he was ashamed of us and that he was going to ask our parents not to come to the game so we wouldn't embarrass them. He ranted along the sidelines and yelled as much at his players as at the officials. Once, when we were supposed to beat Leypoldt with little effort but were behind at halftime, he stomped out of the locker room, announcing he'd sit in the opposing team's rooting section for the rest of the game — and he did. If, over a season, he gave you one compliment, you saved it as though it were a seven-pound gold nugget.

It's not as though the coaches practiced bad coach/good coach to worry and then soothe us. They were genuinely and completely different and had been best friends all their lives. They fulfilled their dreams by returning to Wilhelm as head football coaches. They wanted to be co-head coaches, but the school board said committees seldom coach well, so the title of head coach alternated every year from one to the other. But the way they coached never changed.

That night returning from Elias the other seniors and I could sense that the yearly argument was about to detonate. Sanders and Cronin had grown up in Wilhelm and played football under Coach Van Dyke. Coach Van Dyke came to Wilhelm for their freshmen year. Until then Wilhelm had lost nearly every football game for a decade. By the time Cronin and Sanders were seniors, they played in the state championship game. Once a year, they argued about that game.

I suppose we felt it coming because Mr. Van Dyke's funeral had been that morning. He continued to coach, but for a Double A team 75 miles away (we were Triple A).

"God, he was only 52," Sanders said. "A lot of good it does to stay in shape."

Cronin didn't respond.

Sanders said even louder and higher, "But the poor, old guy had lost it years ago."

"Don't start that again, not today," Cronin said quietly. "He's just fresh in the ground. Let him rest."

"Humf," Sanders said, and folded his arms in an exaggerated manner and shifted his body to look out the window. Within two seconds he turned back toward Cronin. "He should've called a half back dive off left tackle, then maybe a counter next. We had it. It was in our hands. One more first down and we'd have been champs."

"Johnnie, he was young. Remember that. He was 27 years old. We've got him by eight years already."

"He called a reverse though the other team wasn't over-pursuing. In fact, they were penetrating in their lanes like a Rebel charge against Union lines."

"It was different then. We were playing Cro-Magnon football. High school coaches didn't get training — a handful of films, certainly no videos, a couple dozen staple plays. We know ten times what he did."

Sanders turned to the window again. A truck passed. Warren and I saw their faces, jaws rigid, lips rolled tight. It wasn't done. We could tell. Something hung between them like the silence in a World War I trench a minute before the troops went over the top. It wasn't as if the two strongest boys in school were going to fight to see which was the toughest. Since the coaches were there for the sake of us boys, I believe they were like parents deciding to quarrel until they hit a satisfactory conclusion, not simply for the sake of their relationship, but to show their children how to resolve a predicament.

Finally Cronin said, "The press was playing him up: taking the team from worst to first. And the terrible trinity — principal, athletic director, and superintendent of schools — they'd all been coaches. They were sitting on his head for two weeks before the game."

"Listen, Wayne. He was wrong. Why can't you say it? If, in those same circumstances, somebody across the field from us called that play, you'd leap for joy. He made a stupid, stupid call, and we lost the state championship. It's simple."

The bus geared down as we passed through a burg. A tavern's neon sign flashed purple and orange, distorting the coaches' faces with the colors.

"It was a terrible week for him, his mother ill," Cronin said. "If it were me, I couldn't have shown up to play. He got as many players into the game as he could. We made mistakes on the field just as he did from the bench. I simply don't think it's that important."

"You said it. You finally said it. He made a mistake."

"Okay. He made a mistake. I also said it's not important. Maybe if I'd agreed with you years ago, it'd be easier for you to admit what's most important."

"Like what?"

"If we didn't know it when we played, we do now that we coach. He did it for us, not for himself. That's why we leaped off the line with every hike, Johnnie, and why we dove for every tackle, and held our blocks as though defending home and family from the Visigoths. And it's because of Alvie Van Dyke that you and I are coaches, whether we won that damned championship or not. He loved us, every day, every practice, every game. What he did, whether judged foolish or simply uncreative, was done from a heart bursting with love for us. And...."

His throat caught. Warren and I could see Sanders beside him, his face, huge, glowing, angelic in the lights of passing cars. Cronin now looked directly ahead, as though what he'd said was concerning the direction of the bus. Sanders turned squarely to Cronin and just looked at him, a long time, maybe twenty heartbeats. Then he slowly put his arm around Cronin's shoulder and they sat silently, Sanders' arm around Cronin, as the bus rumbled past Hour Glass Lake, and on through Millford, then finally through Druid toward Wilhelm, Sander's arm around Cronin, and each silent as prayer, for the rest of the way home.

As we've agreed before, Pop, life and the Christian faith aren't simple. I didn't figure out all at once what occurred in our presence upon the team bus traveling from Elias to Wilhelm. I didn't go home saying, "Let this be a lesson to me." As I said, I've thought about it off and on for years.

You know, Pop, I respect people who can do things — get theory into practice; and unless it's good theory, it won't work. That night, two decades ago I saw one man who held to the truth and one man who held to love, yet neither truth nor love was adequate alone. It took another man, a man who loved them, to die before together they could finally speak the truth in love. That, to me, seems the balance of Christian morality.

I'm sure you'll have something to say about this. I'll await your response.

Sincerely,
Your son-in-law

Discussion Questions

1. What immediate responses do you have to the story?

2. Do you identify with a character in the story? If yes, how and why do you identify with the person? If no, why don't you identify with anyone in the story?

3. Would you like to have a conversation with a character in the story? What would you say, ask, or suggest to the person? Why?

4. How does the story bring the biblical text into a clearer focus for you?

5. How would you improve or modify the story? Why?

6. How easy is it for you to face the truth about the failings of people you love?

7. What kind of grudge is hardest for you to release? What kinds of things are hardest for you to forgive?

8. In what ways outside the church and conventional Christian training have you learned lessons that contribute to your understanding of Christian morality?

9. What further depths of meaning, symbols, connections with, or applications of the biblical faith do you find in the story?

10. Since Jesus Christ has risen from the dead and is alive among us through his Holy Spirit, what of this story would you like Christ to activate in your life?

Emphasis or special occasion: Seminary Sunday, Ordination, or Installation of Pastor

Chapter 34

Doctor Of Divinity

1 Peter 5:1-4

"Pastors have a particularly difficult set of heartaches, because you must keep confidences, which means you can't reveal the horrible things people have said to you, or sometimes what they've done to you. I'm sure you've been instructed about confidentiality in your classes. I suggest that you maintain confidentiality even beyond the death of those whose confidences you keep."

The Reverend Alexander Curry was addressing the graduating class of his alma mater. One hundred eight seminary students sat row upon row before him. Few knew him personally. Most understood that he wasn't a particularly successful evangelist, powerful preacher, renowned scholar, or prophet for Christ's church. But over the course of his ministry he'd managed to raise more money for the seminary than almost any single person — therefore, the honorary Doctor of Divinity Degree granted him today and his speaking to the graduates.

On the podium sat Dean Landsdorf, a psychosomatic barometer of everything that happened during the graduation ceremonies. He was a pastor before returning to teaching and his was always a pastor's heart. His head was already cocked slightly to the side as if to ask: Is this what graduates need to hear — heartaches and confidentiality?

"Some of your parishioners will demand worship be exactly the same as or exactly the opposite of the way they imagine worship was when they were children," Alexander Curry said. "Some will request worship be a Broadway musical or a Bach recital. Some of your parishioners will expect sermons that inform them about only arcane subjects such as what happened to the Hittites. A few will demand the thinnest of moralistic broth for a sermon. Others would substitute for a sermon a chat, group therapy, drama, or dance."

The dean shifted uncomfortably in his chair as though he didn't need his entire faculty riled by a series of insults.

"I'd like you to ask yourselves," Alexander Curry said, "how do you face a congregation Sunday after Sunday when you can't please everyone, when people resist the ministry you believe you are called and gifted to do, when the heartaches accumulate? How do you make your calls when you're numb from struggling against inertia, not to mention sin, in your congregation? Sin does await you there. All kinds of neuroses wait to focus upon you as a religious authority and to punish you for how a parishioner was or wasn't treated in childhood. How will you counsel and encourage others when you're a magnet for the anger that can't be safely aimed at anyone else, because anyone else would fight back? You'll get used to hearing, 'Pastor, a few of the members are saying....'

"I ask you again, if no one has asked you before and if you haven't asked yourselves: How will you continue Lord's day after Lord's day, Easter after Christmas, living and telling the good news of Jesus Christ to people, of whom some will hurt you — in ways that range from merely erasing a smidgen of your religious dignity to butchering your career?"

Dean Landsdorf lifted his head from his hands, as if thinking, well, maybe he's arrived at something worth saying.

"I won't answer that question," Curry said from behind the lectern, "but I'll tell you about one pastor. Although I'm much concerned with confidentiality, I'll report what happened to this pastor a long time ago and in a different denomination. We'll call him Pastor Michael."

* * *

Michael had served in his first pastorate at St. John's for six months when he walked into the sanctuary one Tuesday morning to find a parishioner standing, fists upon his hips. He swung toward Michael with a giant smile and said, "Pastor Michael, I just retired. What can I do for the church?"

As Michael put it, no loose cannon in a storm ever inflicted more damage upon the deck of a ship than did this man in this congregation. Michael felt guilty about him, because he and his wife referred to him as "Just Great Gary." Gary would meet you anytime, anywhere with a broad smile that broadcast trouble to anyone who could decode superficiality. Ask him how he was and he'd give that smile and say, "Just great. Just great." Michael's wife, Charlene, said that if Gary really was feeling good, he'd tell you three times instead of twice.

Gary told Michael that he'd owned a successful business, was an excellent administrator, and was expert at getting the most from employees. The church board made him chair of the personnel committee.

A few weeks later, Gary was sitting in the secretary's office doing an abbreviated time and motion study. Michael stepped in and felt the tension immediately.

"We're tightening up some work routines here, pastor," Gary said. "Straightening a few procedure lines. In a couple days, Winifred and I'll have streamlined the office into the twenty-first century."

Gary laughed toward Michael, but Michael scrutinized Winifred. He could sense annoyance and insult radiating from her. Just Great Gary came back daily for a week. Winifred began protesting to Michael the third day and by the end of the week was threatening to quit. Michael tried to ignore the severity of the situation and encouraged Winifred to try to learn from Gary, but Winifred complained to the board. The board got Gary to back off a little, but Winifred quit within a year. Michael began the difficult training of a new secretary, more difficult because Winifred quit not only as secretary but also as a church member.

Gary insisted that he take part in training the new secretary, since he could help on some "big picture stuff" about why to be a secretary. This secretary lasted four months. Michael anticipated a revolving door of secretaries, but the third secretary surprised him by staying. She was probably the most incompetent secretary ever to lick a stamp, but she was as impervious to criticism as she was to training. She was also the daughter of the church's largest donor, and no one even considered firing her. After two months of sporadic attempts, Gary gave her up as a lost cause and turned his energy in another direction: sermon critique.

Sunday at the sanctuary door after worship, Michael was shaking hands as people left. Just Great Gary came by, smiling. He shook Michael's hand a little too long saying, "Your second point was feeble. You know: 'When an argument is weak, shout like blazes.' " And he smiled. Michael was bothered, but thought he should let such things go. The following Sunday, there was Gary smiling after worship, "Your final illustration didn't quite fit the conclusion. It needed more snap."

All week, Michael dreaded Sunday. The next Sunday, however, Gary just smiled at the door and Michael thought he'd graduated from sermon boot camp. But that week Gary ambled into Michael's office, sprawled on a chair and said, "Thought maybe we'd talk about next Sunday's sermon."

"Next Sunday's sermon?"

"You need some help. Here." He handed Michael two pages, typed, single-spaced. "Here are some thoughts to consider for next Sunday's sermon."

"But Gary, I've got my texts planned three months ahead."

"Well, I'm here from the congregation to tell you to switch your plans so when you speak, your listeners don't mentally wander. See?"

At about this time Gary began, as he put it, encouraging the choir director, monitoring the treasurer's accounting system, and adjusting the janitor's schedule, and Michael realized what a bind he was in. As obnoxious as Gary seemed on the surface, something even deeper was beginning to erode the spiritual health of the St. John's congregation. Michael had been counseling Gary's wife, Doris, who over the years only attended worship when Gary did, and that wasn't often. She never talked much when Gary was around. Doris confided that she and Gary had quarreled for months. It took Michael a while, but he finally deduced that another woman he was counseling — a much younger woman — was having an affair with Gary.

Michael couldn't share what he knew. Except the few things he could tell Charlene about Gary's bull-in-a-china-shop management skills and his constant criticism of the sermons, Michael couldn't even hint to her why he was now edgy all the time. Michael contacted his district superintendent and acknowledged that he was in far over his head.

His district superintendent agreed that Michael didn't deal well with conflict and didn't have the skills to outmaneuver Just Great Gary. In June, the district superintendent moved Michael and Charlene to a congregation at the other end of the conference and basically gave them a chance to start over in the pastorate. The district superintendent then demonstrated that God had placed him in the right position in the church. He sent a new pastor to St. John's, a second-career pastor who'd formerly owned a business. Sparks flew in his first few months there; but, the new pastor reported that, after some initial resistance, control of the congregation was wrestled from Gary. Gary had some accompanying marital problems, but the new pastor reported that this seemed within acceptable limits. St. John's was able to turn its energy away from Gary and back into ministry.

Michael and Charlene also did well in their new congregation and were there six or seven years, when Charlene suffered severe abdominal pains. The diagnosis of cancer was swift, as was the surgery. She was, by her own estimate, back to 80% horsepower within a few months. Nine weeks after her operation, Gary and Doris phoned Charlene that they were coming to town and wanted to stop by. Charlene was still shaky, but they agreed on a time and she phoned Michael so they could all have coffee together.

Michael was home to greet them. Gary bowed his head slightly as he walked through their front door, and he didn't give his "Just Great" answer when Michael asked how he was. "Fine," he said, and his smile wasn't as full as usual. Doris wore a bright, red dress and chattered about how splendid the weather was for a drive.

Once they were seated, Gary cleared his throat. "Pastor Michael, I ... ah, we, wanted to come when we heard that Charlene had been ill."

Fortunately, he turned toward Charlene as he spoke her name, because if Gary had spoken directly to Michael, Michael wouldn't have known what to say. Charlene spoke a polite and appreciative, "Thank you, Gary. Thank you, Doris."

"And," Gary said, turning to Michael, "I appreciate the time you spent with me at St. John's. I'm thankful you were our pastor through a season that was difficult for both of us. Doris and I are better now, and we each owe you a lot. We decided if we were grateful, we'd better come tell you, especially now. And we needed to tell you we're praying for you both."

"Thank you," Charlene said again, "but I'm afraid my condition was exaggerated when reported to St. John's."

"That's okay with us," Doris said, "Gave us good reason to stop and see you."

They stayed about 45 minutes. The good-byes were pleasant. After Gary and Doris were out the door, Michael and Charlene just stood looking at one another, smiling.

* * *

"Graduates, you are already my brothers and sisters in Christ. Most of you will soon become my colleagues in the pastoral ministry. Problems await you there that you won't be able to fix. You'll get blame and credit that you don't deserve and, if you try to get things done for our Lord Jesus instead of being custodian of a religious museum or director of a religious social club, sometimes you'll receive more blame than credit. Yet, by being faithful, by trying, by being a presence for Christ, something happens, something that after a number of years you can smile about.

"Why would anyone enter such a profession and how could anyone remain in such a profession, unless they possessed some gruesome instinct that made them enjoy suffering? It won't be the salary! You'll need more than sincere motives, good citizenship, and civilized tolerance. You'll require something beyond a solid seminary education and support from colleagues and denomination. You must believe with all your heart that our Lord Jesus suffered for us and still does and that his suffering for us and rising to new life for us is worth all our life in response. Christ's ministry wasn't easy. Our ministry on his behalf isn't easy; but in the end, serving our Lord Jesus Christ is worth more than anything else.

"Receive these words from the apostle Peter's first letter, chapter 5, verses 1-4: 'Now as an elder myself and a witness of the sufferings of Christ, as well as one who shares in the glory to be revealed, I exhort the elders among you to tend the flock of God that is in your charge, exercising the oversight, not under compulsion but willingly, as God would have you do it — not for sordid gain but eagerly. Do not lord it over those in your charge, but be examples to the flock. And when the chief shepherd appears, you will win the crown of glory that never fades away.' "

As the Reverend Alexander Curry, Doctor of Divinity, stepped away from the lectern, Dean Landsdorf was first on the podium to stand and join the graduates, clapping with all his might.

Discussion Questions

1. What immediate responses do you have to the story?

2. Do you identify with a character in the story? If yes, how and why do you identify with the person? If no, why don't you identify with anyone in the story?

3. Would you like to have a conversation with a character in the story? What would you say, ask, or suggest to the person? Why?

4. How does the story bring the biblical text into a clearer focus for you?

5. How would you improve or modify the story? Why?

6. Has God surprised you by bringing health into the lives of others whom you hadn't been able to help?

7. Have you experienced a failure that proved, in the long run, not to be as tragic as it first seemed?

8. If you addressed seminary graduates, what would you tell them from your experience in the Christian faith that would help them remain faithful to Jesus Christ?

9. What further depths of meaning, symbols, connections with, or applications of the biblical faith do you find in the story?

10. Since Jesus Christ has risen from the dead and is alive among us through his Holy Spirit, what of this story would you like Christ to activate in your life?

Emphasis or special occasion: Installation of Pastor or Ordination

Chapter 35

The Most Faithful Nonbeliever

1 John 3:11

Edith Glowacky sang in the church choir for 28 years. She seldom missed a practice or performance. The choir depended upon her. She was the most faithful nonbeliever ever to bear the name "Presbyterian."

When Edith was a child in pre-World War II Georgia, her mother instructed her numberless times to act ladylike. Her mother's constant advice for growing up was, "Hold to the traditions, marry well, and join a good church." Edith had set about doing just those things, even after she met Rob — on leave from army training camp — and even after World War II, when they married and moved to his home state of Oregon.

Edith had difficulty adapting to the North, especially when Rob took out a giant loan and bought a furniture store in a small town, but they were told that Beaverton had growth potential. As a child, Edith never expected to work outside the home, but now she worked in the furniture store. Still, she maintained a dignity. She always wore a dress or a skirt, never slacks. A bridge club member said, "Edith is always fifteen pounds overweight, but leave it to Edith to be adorned with the most attractive extra fifteen pounds in town."

Even though Edith never considered believing in God, she did develop beliefs. She believed in the smell of new furniture, believed in keeping a well-stocked display floor, believed in advertising, believed in counting units upon delivery, and inspecting every surface for damage as it came out of the crate. She also believed in being a gracious hostess, believed in her bridge club, and, in the summer, believed in golf foursomes.

In 1973, Rob and Edith Glowacky burned the mortgage for their furniture store and, although they'd refinanced their house a couple times to expand and remodel, those payments, too, were almost done. By 1973, their two children were grown and gone — their son, Harvey, an investment counselor in Gresham; their daughter, Norma, a secretary engaged to the vice president of the company where she worked.

This should have been when Edith and Rob could work less and enjoy their friends more, but three things happened. First, a mall built half a mile from their store and attracted a Furniture Circus next to it. The Furniture Circus offered prices that the Glowackys couldn't match — not while maintaining their usual staff. The only way to stay in business was for Rob and Edith to work more.

Second, in April of that year, Rob became ill. He had pains one day in the back, the next day in his side. Within two months, his symptoms were baffling a huddle of specialists. In three months, he could no longer work. Edith shuttled between the store and home to care for Rob. He was in and out of hospitals for tests, and, as his strength slowly faded, Edith wondered whether his next hospital stay would be his last. She anticipated and feared it, but didn't speak about it. Rob was exhausted by whatever was attacking him from within. Edith was exhausted by adding Rob's job to her own and tending to a dying husband. During this time, Edith remained faithful to her church. Seldom did she miss Wednesday night choir practice or Sunday morning worship — no matter how weary or miserable she felt.

Third problem: Their congregation's pastor nominating committee gave notice of calling a new pastor ... a woman. When the news was mentioned at choir practice by a member of the pastor nominating committee, Edith said, "Well, let me tell you, Thomas Epstein, no woman will be my pastor. If you value my opinion and that of many members like me, you'll go right back to that committee and change your decision."

Tom Epstein, a musician of perfect rhythm, lowered his music folder as he, at the same time, dropped his jaw.

"But, Edith. But —" Tom stammered.

"No buts, Tom," Edith said. "It's not proper for a woman to be a pastor."

Marian, standing next to them, looked over her half glasses and raised her eyebrow; but, recognizing Edith's tone, she said nothing.

"This is 1973, not 1910," Tom said.

"What're you talking about? Time's no consideration here. What's proper for the congregation is."

Choir members were edging away as Edith raised her voice.

"But I ... I just can't agree," Tom said.

"Then do the honorable thing, and take my dissenting opinion to your committee and express my *grave* concern. I'm sure many members— men *and* women — in our congregation will agree."

Tom was saying, "But Edith —" as Edith flung her choir folder on the chair and lunged from the choir loft.

Tom reported Edith's convictions. The committee discussed Edith's opinion but agreed that they'd made their decision in the spirit of prayer and concern for their congregation and didn't need to deliberate further. They contacted the presbytery's ministerial relations committee and the church's session to call a congregational meeting and to present their candidate.

From the moment the decision was officially announced, Edith, for the first time in 28 years, stopped attending choir practice and worship. Marian visited the store the next week. She found Edith in the office, a strand of hair hanging loosely on her forehead. Marian talked as Edith opened mail and dashed between typewriter and telephone. Marian spoke slowly, having memorized her lines. "I'm really sorry that you're not singing with us, Edith —"

"I won't be singing with you," Edith cut her off. "I can't be part of what I don't believe in."

"Edith, women do everything now."

"But they shouldn't."

"And you're a woman."

"Makes no difference." Edith answered the phone and dismissed Marian with a flip of her wrist.

The following week Albert Selvig, chairman of the pastor nominating committee, telephoned and asked to call at her home and she agreed for him to arrive at 2:30, when Rob usually napped. A tall, second-generation German, Albert always wore a fedora and his eyes always seemed sad. Today his entire face was sad. After the war, the woman he married had emigrated from Germany to the United States. For her first two years in the country, Rob and Edith had sponsored her and given her a job.

"Edith, my good friend," he said from the doorway holding his hat. They shook hands.

"Please come in," she said, leading him to the living room to sit on an overstuffed chair of earth tones. "We'll have to speak quietly, so Rob can sleep."

Edith brought a teapot and cups on a tray and they exchanged pleasantries.

"I've heard you're upset about the pastor nominating committee's choice." Albert kept his voice low. "You've always been so good to Lotti and me; I wanted to explain our decision."

"You don't have to explain anything. I've made up my mind."

"We prayed a lot about who to call," he said quietly and distinctly. "We had several good candidates, but this Deborah —"

"I'm through with the church. Presbyterians have gone too far."

"We did our very best. We read through a hundred dossiers and met with a dozen people. This lady —"

"There's nothing you can say to convince me. Women shouldn't be pastors. If you respect me, I ask that you not mention this again."

She couldn't resist shaking his hand when he left, but her doing so was a formality. He said he'd pray for Rob and her. She thanked him.

Three weeks later, Rob was completely bedridden. Edith had lost twenty pounds. Her dresses hung limply upon her but she had no time to shop for new ones. Business was off 27%. Harvey phoned every evening and stopped by twice a week. Norma canceled the date for her wedding, due to the uncertainty of her father's health.

No one had taken Edith off the church's mailing list, or perhaps someone had told someone to take her off, but someone else continued mailing anyway. Edith opened every letter. One was an announcement that Deborah Keats was now on the field — which meant she was residing as pastor — and inviting the congregation and community to the service of her installation on a Sunday evening five weeks hence. Edith considered the invitation's style of print and thought they could have done better. She tossed it and didn't think again about this woman, Deborah Keats, until three nights later, when Rob woke barely able to breathe.

The ambulance ride was all fear for her and Rob. His eyes were large, his face panicky. He couldn't speak. When the ambulance attendant appeared worried, Edith assured Rob that he'd be all right. He closed his eyes slowly and didn't open them for the rest of the ride. She kept stroking his hand and speaking soothingly to him.

Edith couldn't remain with Rob in the emergency room, but was reunited with him an hour and a half later in intensive care. She kept wondering what else she could do or say, and, if she were to say something, to whom would she say it? By 4:45 a.m., she was sitting hopelessly beside Rob with her head bowed, semi-conscious in the dimly lit room. A woman stepped in. She was short and thick, and she stood near the doorway with the light glowing from behind. She didn't wear a hospital uniform.

"Mrs. Glowacky?"

"Yes?" Edith looked up.

"I'm Pastor Debbie Keats. Albert Selvig phoned that your husband came by ambulance to the hospital."

She moved closer to Edith so the light behind her wasn't as blinding. Edith could make out her salt-and-pepper hair. When Edith heard that Albert had sent her, she expected to get mad. Instead she said, "How do you do."

Edith held up her right hand. Debbie Keats reached out both hands. Edith was weak and she felt the pastor's grasp like a gentle, religious death grip, but she was without energy to pull away. Then she realized that she didn't want to pull away. Edith's left hand remained upon Rob, her right hand secure in the warm, small embrace of a woman pastor whom she'd never known, but opposed.

"Albert said you're his dear friend and he owes you a great debt. He couldn't rest until I came to see you."

Edith looked up into this trusting face and assumed that Albert told her nothing except that Edith and Rob were in need. All she could say was, "That Albert."

In the subdued light, they held hands for a few minutes, listening to Rob breathe. Occasionally, he grunted. Debbie said softly, "Would you like me to pray?"

Edith hesitated only half a second, "Yes, please."

Debbie took her right hand from Edith's and placed it upon Rob's hand and in about fifty words uttered a prayer for health, for mercy, for strength, and for faith. Nothing fancy, only that her entire heart and life flowed out in her words to God.

In the next week, Rob had his setbacks, but he was out of intensive care in five days and home from the hospital in two weeks. Three weeks later he was able to visit work and sit in the office a couple hours a day.

On the Sunday evening of Pastor Keats' installation, the sanctuary filled. The congregation and choir sang grand songs of faith. Two neighboring pastors and an elder spoke; and, after Debbie Keats was called forward to answer the constitutional questions, the elder administering her vows turned to the congregation. "To inaugurate the Reverend Keats' ministry here, would the pastor nominating committee along with presbytery's commission come forward to lay hands upon her for prayer." As an afterthought, he scanned the congregation and said, "And if anyone else would like to take part in this prayer, come also and join the party." He smiled broadly and the congregation laughed.

Around the congregation a few people began to rise and walk forward to the small group circling the kneeling minister. Edith Glowacky hurried a little faster than others and found her way to the side of Albert Selvig. They joined hands to pray beside their new pastor, the Reverend Deborah Keats.

Discussion Questions

1. What immediate responses do you have to the story?

2. Do you identify with a character in the story? If yes, how and why do you identify with the person? If no, why don't you identify with anyone in the story?

3. Would you like to have a conversation with a character in the story? What would you say, ask, or suggest to the person? Why?

4. How does the story bring the biblical text into a clearer focus for you?

5. How would you improve or modify the story? Why?

6. Does your religious tradition encourage or prevent women as pastors? Do you respond differently to male and female pastors?

7. What are some nonessential traditions from your youth that are hard for you to break from?

8. Has someone's loving ministry to you changed what you believed or contributed to the health of your loved ones?

9. What further depths of meaning, symbols, connections with, or applications of the biblical faith do you find in the story?

10. Since Jesus Christ has risen from the dead and is alive among us through his Holy Spirit, what of this story would you like Christ to activate in your life?

Chapter 36

Seeing The End

Revelation 1:4b-8

"At least the preacher wasn't too religious," James said. He pouched out his cheeks as was his older brother manner when speaking the summary of his thoughts.

"And he pronounced 'Smythe' correctly," Dorie said. "Better than that preacher at Aunt Wilma's funeral." She sat at the kitchen table, looking right and left as she spoke to her two brothers. The early evening wind blew hard against the house. Everyone else had left the reception at their father's home. Just the three grown children now, without their spouses, in the kitchen of their dead parents' home.

James and Dorie looked at Phil because, by a lifetime of practice, it was now his turn in the rotation to comment on their father's funeral. Dorie tapped her foot under the kitchen table. James remained standing, arms crossed, back against the refrigerator.

Beside the kitchen window, Phil watched the wind strip the last leaves from their parents' giant cherry tree. He was 35 and the youngest. He chewed his gum slowly. His sister and brother waited as they listened to the breeze.

Although Phil was next in the siblings' order to speak, James, deciding to wait no longer, coughed and offered another observation. "And the music wasn't as bad as I feared." He ended the sentence on an upturn, for Phil to pick up the conversation; but Phil furrowed his forehead with a deeper look of concentration to his gum chewing.

"I think Mom would have liked it," Dorie said, tapping her foot now against the leg of the kitchen table. She turned again to Phil as though handing a baton. But the room fell silent. After two or three minutes, James said, "Come on, Phil." He held out his arms toward Phil. "What did you think of Dad's funeral?"

Phil moved a step toward them, although still half turned to the window. The wind pushed a few drops of rain sideways against the glass. He spoke quietly, "Dad kept saying he wanted to see the end of the building project."

"Absolutely," James said. "He was fixated on it. Even when I was here a month ago and he'd entered the hospital for the first time, he said, 'I want to see the end of it.' "

Their father had taken the chairmanship of the church's fund-raising for a new building. The congregation raised the money and the construction of the gym and classroom complex was nearly complete.

"I'm amazed he got into the religion stuff at all," Dorie said. "He never even talked about church when we were kids. I think neighbors took him to church after Mom died."

"Well, they saw his abilities real fast," James said. "They threw him into the chairmanship after only a couple years. 'I've got to see the end of it,' he'd say. Like he was obsessed. I thought maybe in the last month he had a little stroke thrown into his heart problems."

Phil slowed chewing his gum and said, "I was able to drive and visit him once a week in the last month before he died, and he had graphs and charts and blueprints all over the house. He was pretty sincere about it. 'I got it started. I want to see the end of it.' Seems that's all he could think of."

"But the service," Dorie said, bringing them back to the subject at hand.

"It was short enough," James said as he laughed, "even though the preacher wandered from beginning to end. He seemed like the cowboy who jumped on his horse and rode off in all directions."

"But he made such a big deal out of Dad's peace at the end," Dorie said. "Even when he read from that Revelations book."

"He was trying to make a point, I could tell," James said. "It sailed over me, and I think over everybody. Who reads Revelations at a funeral? Pretty baffling stuff: alpha, omega."

"I think he said that seven times in seven minutes," Dorie said, "and each time talking about how calm Dad had been during the last week."

"That he was," James said. "In fact, a couple times when I was with him in the hospital he smiled and cried at the same time. He wasn't upset. I'm sure, even though he couldn't talk well. And like a recording he mentioned the end again. The last thing he mumbled was that he'd seen the end. And he smiled. I guess I hadn't told you two that."

"No," Dorie said, "you hadn't. He smiled? Said he'd seen the end?"

Phil chewed his gum harder, brow wrinkled, nearly a frown. "That Revelation the pastor read." Dorie and James nodded their heads. "The alpha and omega he kept repeating."

"Those are Greek letters," James said. "I wondered when he read it if that's why fraternities got Greek letters."

Phil stopped chewing his gum, "Well, alpha and omega are the beginning and end of the Greek alphabet. And the Bible said that God was the alpha and the omega."

Dorie's foot stopped. Her eyes became very wide. "So God's the beginning," she said as she turned to James, who spoke slowly, "and Dad saw the end."

Discussion Questions

1. What immediate responses do you have to the story?

2. Do you identify with a character in the story? If yes, how and why do you identify with the person? If no, why don't you identify with anyone in the story?

3. Would you like to have a conversation with a character in the story? What would you say, ask, or suggest to the person? Why?

4. How does the story bring the biblical text into a clearer focus for you?

5. How would you improve or modify the story? Why?

6. Have you and your siblings discussed your parents' faith? If you don't have siblings, have you spoken of your parents' faith with relatives?

7. Did you figure out important things about your parents' or relatives' lives and faith after they died?

8. Has a loved one's dying brought you to a fuller understanding of God?

9. What further depths of meaning, symbols, connections with, or applications of the biblical faith do you find in the story?

10. Since Jesus Christ has risen from the dead and is alive among us through his Holy Spirit, what of this story would you like Christ to activate in your life?

Scripture Index

Genesis 2:7, 18-25	Chapter 1
Genesis 28:10-12	Chapter 21
Exodus 12:1-4	Chapter 2
Exodus 12:11-14	Chapter 2
Deuteronomy 26:1-11	Introduction
2 Samuel 1:1-17	Chapter 3
1 Kings 8:22-30	Chapter 4
1 Kings 8:41-43	Chapter 4
Job 38:1-7	Chapter 5
Psalm 125:2	Chapter 11
Isaiah 9:2	Chapter 6
Isaiah 9:6	Chapter 23
Isaiah 53:7-8	Chapter 11
Hosea 11:3	Chapter 7
Matthew 2:1-12	Chapter 8
Matthew 5:38-39	Chapter 9
Mark 1:21-28	Chapter 10
Mark 1:40-44	Chapter 11
Mark 4:10-12	Chapter 12
Mark 9:30-37	Chapter 13
Mark 12:28-34	Chapter 14
Mark 15:21-26	Chapter 15
Luke 6:17-26	Chapter 16
Luke 21:25-36	Chapter 17

Luke 22:54-66	Chapter 18
Luke 23:50-56	Chapter 19
Luke 24:36-48	Chapter 20
John 1:43-51	Chapter 21
John 2:13-22	Chapter 22
John 3:6-8	Chapter 23
John 6:1-21	Chapter 24
John 11:1-13, 38-44	Chapter 25
John 21:20-25	Chapter 26
Acts 7:2-53	Introduction
1 Corinthians 2:12	Chapter 27
1 Corinthians 8:1-13	Chapter 28
1 Corinthians 13	Chapter 29
2 Corinthians 11:29	Chapter 30
Galatians 3:28	Chapter 31
Ephesians 3:14-19	Chapter 32
Ephesians 4:15-16	Chapter 33
1 Peter 5:1-4	Chapter 34
1 John 3:11	Chapter 35
Jude 24-25	Chapter 12
Revelation 1:4b-8	Chapter 36

Emphasis Or Special Occasion Index

Baccalaureate	Chapter 7
Christmas	Chapter 23
Christmas Eve	Chapter 6
Church conflict	Chapter 29
Doubt	Chapter 21
Epiphany	Chapter 8
Ethics, Christian	Chapter 28
Faith	Chapter 30
Father's Day	Chapter 32
Football	Chapter 33
Good Friday	Chapter 18
Graduation	Chapter 7
Grief	Chapter 3
Independence Day	Chapter 9
Installation of Pastor	Chapter 34, 35
Lord's Supper, The	Chapter 24
Marriage	Chapter 1
Martin Luther King Day	Chapter 31
Maundy (Holy) Thursday	Chapter 2, 18
Ordination	Chapter 27; 34, 35
Prayer	Chapter 12
Resurrection Sunday	Chapter 15, 19, 20, 25
Seminary Sunday	Chapter 34
Thanksgiving	Chapter 31

www.ingramcontent.com/pod-product-compliance
Lightning Source LLC
Chambersburg PA
CBHW070547160426
43199CB00014B/2401